Fannie Hochstetler

for thou art
with me

for thou art with me

◆ ◆ ◆

The Healing Power of Psalms

Samuel Chiel and Henry Dreher

An Imprint of Rodale Books

© 2000 by Samuel Chiel and Henry Dreher
Cover and interior photographs © by Y. Campanella/Panoramic Images, Chicago

Cover and Interior Designer: Christopher Rhoads
Cover and Interior Photographer: Y. Campanella/Panoramic Images, Chicago

All Psalms except Psalm 23 reprinted from *Tanakh: The Holy Scriptures* © 1985 by the Jewish Publication Society. Used by permission.

Library of Congress Cataloging-in-Publication Data

Chiel, Samuel.
    For Thou art with me : the healing power of Psalms / Samuel Chiel and Henry Dreher.
        p.   cm.
    ISBN 1–57954–176–3   hardcover
    1. Bible. O.T. Psalms—Criticism, interpretation, etc.   2. Spiritual healing.   3. Healing—Religious aspects—Judaism.   I. Dreher, Henry. II. Title.
BS1430.6.H39 C45   2000
223'.206—dc21   00–024083

Distributed to the book trade by St. Martin's Press

2 4 6 8 10 9 7 5 3 1   hardcover

Visit us on the Web at www.rodalebooks.com, or call us toll-free at (800) 848-4735.

To the memory of

Rabbi Arthur A. Chiel
Dr. Bernard Eisenberg
Malka Levine

The righteous are called living, even after death.
—The Talmud

CONTENTS

◆   ◆   ◆

PRAYERS FOR HEALING

SPIRITUAL COPING

ACCEPTANCE AND RECOVERY

ACKNOWLEDGMENTS

◆ ◆ ◆

I am grateful to a number of people for their help in the process of writing this book.

To my beloved brother, Rabbi Arthur A. Chiel, of blessed memory, who was a great rabbi and scholar and an outstanding human being. Some years ago, he and Rabbi Edward Sandrow prepared a pamphlet of prayers and readings for people who were ill, entitled *Foundation of Life*, which was published by the Rabbinical Assembly. Rabbis continue to distribute this pamphlet to patients, who have found it invaluable. This book is a continuation of his work on behalf of people who are ill or in crisis, who need spiritual strength to face their ordeals.

I am grateful to the people whose stories I tell and who have inspired me by their courage and faith. One of them, Edwin Kolodny, M.D., of the New York University Medical Center in New York City, allowed me to reprint portions of a letter he wrote to me, and I thank him for that and for his inspiration. I also thank Ivy and Becky Feuerstadt for sharing their story as well.

I am indebted to my coauthor (and nephew) Henry Dreher, who has been a wonderful partner in writing this book. I am also grateful to his wife, my niece, Deborah Chiel, for her helpful advice and counsel in the process of creation.

And I thank my wonderful wife, Janet. I am grateful to her for each day of our life together and for her unfailing wisdom, strength, and love, which sustain me always.

—Samuel Chiel

We wish to thank our agents, Chris Tomasino and Jonathan Diamond, for the wonderful work they have done on our behalf, work that has enabled *For Thou Art with Me* to become a reality.

We are most grateful to our superb editor, Christian

Millman, who has been enthusiastic, available, and helpful throughout the editorial process and beyond. We also thank others at Rodale and Daybreak who have supported this project: Neil Wertheimer, Hugh O'Neill, and Cindy Ratzlaff. We reserve special mention for Karen Kelly, whose initial interest in the project made it possible.

Terese Brown, transcriber extraordinaire, did an excellent job and was, as always, a positive and supportive presence.

Naomi Chiel deserves special mention for her effervescent enthusiasm about our project and for her creative and vigorous efforts on the book's behalf. We also thank Kinneret Chiel for her steadfast support of our project from the very start.

Several individuals have lent their support to this project and done so publicly in a way that we deeply appreciate: Larry Dossey, M.D.; Jerome Groopman, M.D.; Sherwin Nuland, M.D.; and Bernie Siegel, M.D. These physicians have led the way toward a humanistic, spiritually evolved medicine, and their contributions have been so significant that we may not fully comprehend them for decades.

—Samuel Chiel and Henry Dreher

I wish to thank Larry LeShan, Ph.D., whose heartfelt, wide-eyed reaction to my very first description of this project was like a beam of light that I rode to the book's completion. I am also grateful to Bill Thomson, editor of *Natural Health* magazine, who not only offered his strong support but also instantly quoted Psalms from memory that we ended up using in the book.

Special thanks go to my wife, Deborah Chiel, for her unbelievably astute feedback, her endless support, and her love. I thank her as well for bringing me into the family whose energy and belief form the core of *For Thou Art with Me*. Finally, I wish to thank my coauthor, my uncle Samuel Chiel, a man of wisdom and genuine compassion, a spiritual leader in the truest sense of that description—a real rarity. He has also been an unfailingly supportive, patient, and easygoing partner in the writing process. That, too, is a rarity.

—Henry Dreher

Authors' Note

◆ ◆ ◆

Although *For Thou Art with Me* is a collaborative effort by Samuel Chiel and Henry Dreher, for the sake of clarity and simplicity we decided to use the pronoun *I* throughout, for Samuel Chiel, particularly because many of the stories in the book are derived from Rabbi Chiel's experiences with members of his congregation and others.

For Thou Art with Me includes commentaries on 15 Psalms, a few of which are presented in their entirety. Most, however, have been excerpted to include verses that relate to issues of healing, recovery, and faith in God in the midst of crisis. We did not include verses that we believed would be inappropriate for people or their loved ones who are dealing with severe illness.

You'll also notice that the phrasing of certain lines differs when we're discussing the Psalms. That's because we used the traditional or familiar wording when we felt it better explained the essence of our discussion.

For those wishing to read the full text of these and other Psalms, we relied upon translations from *Tanakh: The Holy Scriptures* (Jewish Publication Society, 1985), though, of course, you may seek out any one of the vast variety of fine translations.

INTRODUCTION

◆　◆　◆

INTRODUCTION

◆　◆　◆

Why a Book of Psalms for Healing?

As a rabbi with more than 40 years of experience, I have advised countless members of my congregations who have suffered with painful and life-threatening illnesses. I have seen them through the cyclic phases of coping: shock, denial, anger, depression, revitalization, renewal, recovery, decline, and death. I have comforted families as they, too, struggled to manage their feelings while trying to help their loved ones through their travails. Often, the most difficult passage for these families is the acute sense of loss that accompanies the death of a loved one. I have offered emotional support for patients and families in all of these circumstances. And I have endeavored to help them find sources of hope and meaning through religious faith.

I have frequently been asked by patients and their families: "What books can I read to help me through this?"

"Where can I turn when I am alone with my fear and sorrow?" I have always felt that they wanted something to hold on to, something clear and explicit that spoke to their deeply held yearnings for solace as they endured tragic circumstances. They wanted a book, in essence, that could help them find their way to God.

Rarely have I felt satisfied with any of the religious or self-help books written to help people in these predicaments. I could recommend the Torah—the first five books of the Bible, which form the cornerstone of Jewish tradition—but I know that most of my congregants, save the most learned or observant, might not delve deeply into these texts in search of succor.

Several years ago, when I myself became ill, I recognized how the Psalms, if presented properly, could fill this need. I was struck with fear when my doctors told me that my heart disease was so serious that I would require triple bypass surgery. I will always remember the moment when the surgeon asked me to sign a permission form listing the many ghastly risks associated with open-heart surgery. Anyone who has signed such a form knows that it highlights only the worst-case scenarios, but the reality of what could happen is still terrifying. I signed the form but was filled with apprehension about what might occur once the anesthetic lulled me into unconsciousness.

But I was able to handle the fear, in part because I had the love of my family and friends. I also had Psalm 30, a beautiful ode to resilience and recovery. One single verse, in its beloved traditional rendering, became my mantra: "Weeping may linger for the night; but joy comes in the morning." The verse reminded me that my suffering was transitory, that joy would be possible in the morning—if not the next morning, then another one soon afterward. These simple words sustained me through my anguish, before and after surgery.

Throughout my protracted and difficult healing process, Psalm 30 bolstered my faith that joy would come in the morning. My convalescence was slow, but it was steady, and in time, I was able to return to my congregation and continue my communal activities.

One might ask why it is important to turn to the Book of Psalms, or to any other liturgical text, in search of prayers for healing. Can we not create our own words of prayer, words that speak to our own particular needs and wishes? Of course we can. But a religious liturgy can vibrate with special meaning and historical resonance. In his book *Man's Quest for God*, the great Jewish scholar

Abraham Joshua Heschel wrote, "It is more inspiring to let the heart echo the music of the ages than to play upon the broken flutes of our own hearts." And the Psalms are nothing if not the music of the ages.

I have long believed in the value of presenting the Psalms to suffering readers in a way that brings them home with immediacy, unfettered by long passages unrelated to healing. My late brother, Rabbi Arthur Chiel, together with Rabbi Edward Sandrow, once compiled a small booklet of Psalms and Jewish prayers relevant to healing that was published under the auspices of the Rabbinical Assembly. Over the past 20 years, I have been amazed by the continuing demand for this pocket-size compendium, as patients and families spread the word that we had a book developed specifically for people in their circumstances.

This booklet is no longer available, and *For Thou Art with Me* will go far beyond the scope of this booklet to fill the need for a book of prayer for healing. It is the book that I have always wanted to hand to congregants, strangers, family members, friends—anyone of any faith who asks me, "What can I read to help me through this?" "Where can I turn when I am alone with my fear and sorrow?"

What We Find in the Psalms

With their lyrical expressions of faith, their powerful imagery, and their uninhibited evocation of passionate feeling, the Psalms speak to people in every imaginable crisis. These universal qualities have made the Book of Psalms a central part of daily worship for Jews and Christians across the ages, and people from other cultural and religious backgrounds have certainly come to treasure the Psalms as literature and as sources of spiritual sustenance.

Slightly fewer than half of the Psalms are directly attributed to King David of Israel. Other Psalms were purportedly written by other seminal figures in Jewish and biblical history—Moses, Solomon, Asaph (a leader of King David's choir), and the sons of Korakh (singers in the temple), among others. While rabbinic scholars have built a tradition around David as the original Psalmist, some modern historians suggest that the Psalms were written by David and other poets beginning in the 10th century before the Common Era (B.C.E.) and spanning many centuries thereafter.

Whether or not the Psalms attributed to King David

were actually composed by him, the Psalms as a whole are imbued with the spirit of David as he is depicted in biblical prose texts. David was a poet and musician, a master and perhaps creator of musical instruments. A man of deep spirituality, David was considered the sweet singer of Israel, and his lyrical gifts are believed by many to have informed his composition of the Psalms. Indeed, many Psalms were meant to be sung and accompanied by instruments. Psalm 150 sings its praise to God in a symphonic blending of sound, with each verse a direction for the use of a new musical instrument: horn, harp, timbrel, lute, pipe, and cymbals.

The poetic and musical qualities of the Psalms help explain some of their ability to stir the soul. But the words themselves tap the deepest dimensions of human spirituality. As biblical scholar Nahum Sarna has written in *On the Book of Psalms*:

> In the Psalms, the human soul extends itself beyond its confining, sheltering, impermanent house of clay. It strives for contact with the Ultimate Source of Life. It gropes for an experience of the divine Presence. The biblical Psalms are essentially a record of the human quest for God. . . . No wonder that they infuse and inform the basic patterns of

both Jewish and Christian worship, give character and essence to their respective liturgies, and govern the life of prayer and spiritual activity of the individual and the congregation.

While the Psalms hold a central place in Judeo-Christian traditions, they have a special meaning for anyone who is sick or suffering. The person who turns to the Psalms in a time of grave illness, or when a loved one is terribly sick, may be lifted up simultaneously by their musical rhythms and their words. In the Psalms, we find words of praise and petition, invocation and despair, anger and acceptance, joy and thanksgiving. And when I suggest to people who are ill or grieving that they turn to the Psalms for support, we know that the words are not simply appropriate to them in their time and place. They are millennial sources of comfort—words that have brought solace and healing to generations.

Years ago, one of my congregants was a renowned pianist who was struck by a debilitating disease, Guillain-Barré syndrome. The illness left him partially paralyzed, unable to play his instrument. When I visited him in the hospital, he broke down in tears as he expressed his terror that he would never regain sufficient use of his hands to return to the piano. He would require months of hospitalization, and it was not clear whether he would ever regain normal use of his extremities, let alone the capacity to play his instrument. I sat and listened as he vented his fear and despair. Then I mentioned a verse from Psalm 89 that I believed might be helpful: "My hand shall be constantly with him, and My arm shall strengthen him."

I suggested to the pianist that he adopt this verse as his own, reciting it when he awoke in the morning and before he went to sleep. I also urged him to say the verse to himself whenever he became overwhelmed by feelings of hopelessness. I went so far as to write the verse on a card in both Hebrew (which he could read) and English. As the poet Mark Van Doren once said, "You must not delight in [the Book of Psalms] occasionally. Don't go to it when you feel some aesthetic impulse and say, 'Oh, isn't that a nice passage.' This is something that must be your constant companion. The repetition isn't merely a repetition, it is a reinforcement."

The pianist listened respectfully as I made my suggestions, but he did not hide his skepticism, saying that my idea was well-intentioned but probably useless. Nevertheless, the next time I visited him, he admitted that he had begun to recite the verse to himself, and much to his surprise, he had found it comforting. The notion that somehow God's arm might strengthen his own had touched him in a profound way.

Gradually, the pianist's condition improved, and after many months of hospitalization, he returned home. On the day of his return, he called me and said, "Rabbi, this verse is now a part of me; it will never leave me. I wanted to recite it to you on my first day home and tell you that without my family, my doctors, and 'my' verse, I could never have made it." We were both moved to tears as he repeated to me over the phone: "My hand shall be constantly with him, and My arm shall strengthen him." I suggested that he now add a time-honored Jewish blessing for moments of great joy: "Blessed are You, Lord our God, who has kept us in life, sustained us, and enabled us to reach this day." In time, the pianist was able to sit down and play his instrument, and eventually, his facility returned. He is once again delighting audiences with his exceptional musical gifts.

One might wonder why people with abiding faith in God would feel compelled to return again and again to the Psalms, but even the most devout can have their beliefs tested under extreme conditions.

Natan Sharansky, the Israeli minister of the interior and

a hero to Jews in Israel and around the world, was imprisoned during the 1970s by Soviet authorities for being a Jewish activist. After nearly 9 years in an infamous labor camp, living under the harshest imaginable conditions, he was finally set free in 1986. When he was released, Sharansky declared that during his imprisonment he had turned to the Book of Psalms to ease his anguish. The Psalms had given him the hope and courage to endure during his most terrifying and dispiriting times in the gulag. Sharansky specifically cited Psalm 27, and we can only assume that in the throes of despair he contemplated the final verse: "Look to the Lord; be strong and of good courage! O look to the Lord!" Upon his arrival in Israel, friends and admirers carried him to Jerusalem's Western Wall to pray and celebrate his emancipation. Onlookers observed that Sharansky was still holding tight to his beloved Book of Psalms.

Just recently, Oprah Winfrey described how she had turned to the Psalms, and particularly to Psalm 27, while in the midst of crisis. During her 6-week trial on charges of maligning the beef industry on her talk show, Winfrey was under attack by powerful plaintiffs. With her reputation and freedom of speech issues on the line, she took the stand on her own behalf. No doubt she found particular solace in these verses from Psalm 27: "Do not subject me to the will of my foes, for false witnesses and unjust accusers have appeared against me. Had I not the assurance that I would enjoy the goodness of the Lord in the land of the living . . . "

President Bill Clinton's mettle has certainly been tested by global crises and personal scandals. Since his election, he seems to have been in a perpetual wrangle with media critics, prosecutors, and political adversaries. In early 1993, under particularly harsh attack, President Clinton revealed that he had read the entire Book of Psalms and that five in particular had brought him relief. (Psalms 25, 27, 90, 103, and 139 were the president's choices; each has strikingly political themes.) Perhaps he found perspective in Psalm 90: "The span of our life is seventy years, or, given the strength, eighty years; but the best of them are trouble and sorrow. They pass by speedily, and we fly away." Life is short, and so is any president's tenure, and the slings and arrows of outrageous fortune will soon cease. But what is the deeper message of Psalm 90? The very next verse provides the answer: "Teach us to count our days rightly, that we may obtain a wise heart."

The universal theme of Psalm 90 carries profound meaning for people who are sick or grieving. How many trees have been sacrificed for self-help books that spin out the same theme with less eloquence and economy? While we must all learn to "count our days rightly, that we may obtain a wise heart," there is something uniquely stirring about reciting these timeless words, knowing that we are connected to generations who have turned to these same verses. As poet and author Kathleen Norris has written in her introduction to a recent publication, *The Psalms*, "When one sits alone with a Psalm, one is sitting with and for the countless others who are praying them now, who have prayed them for thousands of years."

No Psalm is as renowned and often recited—and few others are as comforting to the infirm and the grieving—as Psalm 23. It is beloved by Jews and Christians alike, regardless of sect or sensibility. And with good reason: It is pure poetry to rival Shakespeare or Shelley, and it evokes the timeless belief that God is with us during times of unimaginable torment; as we stare death in the face; at the moment of death; or, perhaps, beyond the borders of death: "Yea, though I walk through the valley of the shadow of death, I will fear no evil: for Thou art with me."

This invocation of God's eternal presence has made Psalm 23 the most beloved in the Book of Psalms. For people with heart disease, cancer, AIDS, or any life-threatening disease, "For Thou art with me" is a quintessential mantra. During moments of quiet reflection and recitation, it imparts the experience of connectedness with the Almighty—the sense that no matter how sick, frightened, or close to death, we are not alone. And for people who are losing or have lost a loved one, it serves as a reminder that we can survive and transcend even the most searing grief.

What we find in Psalm 23 is also what we find in dozens of other Psalms: a cauldron into which we can pour our pains and fears, and from which we receive a revitalized faith, born of the promise of an eternally protective God. In a powerfully direct way, Psalm 121 captures this luminous omnipresence:

> ✗ The Lord is your guardian,
>   the Lord is your protection
>   at your right hand.
> By day the sun will not strike you,
>   nor the moon by night.
> The Lord will guard you from all harm;
>   He will guard your life.
> The Lord will guard your going and coming
>   now and forever. ✗

How to Use the Psalms for Healing

Turning to the Psalms as a form of prayer when we are sick, scared, or grieving will almost surely give comfort. But does it offer more than that? In his marvelous books *Healing Words* and *Prayer Is Good Medicine*, Larry Dossey, M.D., of Santa Fe, New Mexico, documented evidence that prayer can actually heal. He described scores of controlled laboratory studies that prayer, or prayerlike states of empathy or love, can bring about healthful changes in living organisms, from bacteria to humans. "This does not mean that prayer always works, any more than drugs and surgery always work," comments Dr. Dossey. "But . . . statistically speaking, prayer is effective."

Consider the most famous of the prayer studies. In the mid-1980s, cardiologist Randolph Byrd, M.D., of the University of California, San Francisco, randomly assigned 393 patients hospitalized with heart disease to one of two groups, making sure that both groups had similarly severe disease. The first group received "intercessory prayer," which means that they were prayed for by individuals outside the hospital. The second group did not receive such prayer. Neither the patients nor the doctors directing the study knew who was being prayed for. At the study's completion, Dr. Byrd discovered that the prayed-for patients did better on several counts. They required significantly less ventilator support and fewer resuscitations; they had less need for antibiotic and diuretic drugs; and they experienced fewer lung complications. Overall, they had more favorable hospital stays than those who did not receive intercessory prayer. There were also slightly fewer deaths among those who were prayed for by people outside the hospital.

While not without minor methodological flaws, Dr. Byrd's study was still a highly rigorous exploration of intercessory prayer. His results suggest that praying for the health of others is more than a religiously sanctioned exercise in magical thinking: It can make a difference. Other research suggests that people who pray for themselves also experience health benefits. But no research demonstrates that prayer is a surefire cure for any disease.

Such studies challenge our simplistic ideas about God, spirituality, health, and medicine. We are not able to summon a higher power to fix our ailments as though calling upon a faultless repairman. Nor, apparently, are we powerless when we seek divine intercession on our behalf or on behalf of loved ones. These studies suggest that when we open ourselves to the possibilities of prayer, we should cultivate hope without fixed expectations. If we interpret this research to mean that prayer *should* cure, when we are *not* cured we will either conclude that we have not prayed properly or that prayer is bunk altogether. Both of these ideas are potential traps. The first trap implies that we are spiritually dumb or impoverished. Either we haven't prayed correctly or we must not be good enough to deserve divine intervention. The second trap implies that there is no compassionate God to whom we can turn, no source of spiritual sustenance outside of ourselves.

When we analyze statistical findings from the prayer studies, we don't find simple cause-and-effect relationships between prayer and healing. What we find are meaningful trends. These trends reveal that something happens psychologically and physically when we find deeply personal words to ask for help from a God in whom we can believe. Whether the explanation for these happenings is biochemical, emotional, or spiritual, the effect is real. But it is not utterly predictable. Why would it be? Whenever we delve into questions about the worldly effects of prayer, one thing we should count on is mystery. "To pray is to take notice of the wonder, to regain a sense of the mystery that animates all beings, the divine margin in all attainments," writes Heschel in *Man's Quest for God*. "Prayer is our humble answer to the inconceivable surprise of living. It is all we can offer in return for the mystery by which we live."

How can we avoid becoming spurned believers, saddled with self-doubt, or nonbelievers with nowhere to turn in the realm of spirit? How can we take prayer to heart without risking disillusionment and despair? Michael Lerner, Ph.D., head of Commonwealth, a health and environmental research institute, and a leader in the field of complementary medicine, offers a compelling answer in the form of a liberating distinction: Curing and healing are not one and the same. *Cure* refers to the complete physical resolution of a disease. *Healing* may involve physical cure, but it is vastly more encompassing. *Healing* refers to a psychological and spiritual regeneration after we have been wounded, whatever the nature of the wound. Those who cultivate healing might also find that they are cured, usually with the inestimable aid of modern medicine. Or they might not be cured. But regardless of the medical outcome, this broader healing is a goal worth all of our energies—and our prayers.

The notion that healing can occur in the absence of physical cure is perhaps best exemplified by people who find ultimate solace and resolution as they approach death.

As a rabbi, I have witnessed and at times assisted people who experienced the most profound healings during the months and weeks before their deaths. I once counseled a highly successful middle-aged businessman who had battled cancer but had reached a point where physical cure was impossible. Nelson was overwhelmed at the prospect of leaving behind his wife, Ivy, and their three children. As he became increasingly weaker, his depression deepened. A wise psychiatrist advised Nelson to make the best of his time by doing one meaningful thing every day with each of his children. I affirmed the value of this advice, framing it in terms offered by Psalm 90: "Teach us to count our days rightly, that we may acquire a heart of wisdom."

Nelson took our counsel to heart, making sure to watch an inning or two of baseball with his son, Gabe, a devoted fan of the game, or to talk with his daughters, Becky and Samantha, about their schoolwork. But one of his great sorrows was that he would not be present at Becky's bat mitzvah. Halachah (Jewish law) dictates that boys should not undergo this momentous rite of passage until their 13th birthday, and girls may do so at 12. Although Becky was several months from her 12th birthday, I felt that Nelson's wish was so important that we should find a way to honor it, even if it meant bending the rules a bit.

He was far too sick to travel to the synagogue, so I suggested that we hold the bat mitzvah ceremony at the family home. With Nelson confined to a couch, Becky conducted the service with 25 friends and family members in attendance. Nelson was able to fulfill his desire to say the traditional blessing over the Torah during his daughter's reading. As Becky began reciting her Torah portion, she burst into tears and fled the room. A close family friend followed after to comfort her, and soon she returned and flawlessly completed the Torah reading. The spirit in the room was alternately one of sorrow and joyous exultation. Nelson himself was overcome with bittersweet emotion, but he was not deprived of seeing his daughter move toward womanhood. One of the most emotional rituals in which I have been privileged to participate, this bat mitzvah was a passage for both daughter and father, an authentic instance of what author Stephen Levine calls "healing into death."

Thus, if we approach the Psalms as sources of hope for healing—but without rigid expectations of cure—we will not suffer self-blame or spiritual disillusionment should we be unable to rid ourselves of disease. Of course, there should be no reluctance to pray for a physical cure; doing so might even help us to achieve recovery. But, as Buddhist philosophers have helped us to understand, we do well to hold lightly to such expectations. While we may petition God to safeguard the body, it is best to remember that the body is a holy though impermanent vessel, the substance but not the essence of who we are. Perhaps we can use the Psalms as conduits for our request that God safeguard the soul, holding hope that the body will also be protected and revitalized in the process.

Asking God to safeguard the soul and protect the body does not, however, relieve us of responsibility for our healing. We ideally engage in an active rather than passive faith, in which we solicit God's help to mobilize our intelligence and energy in the service of healing. Heschel made this case cogently in *Man's Quest for God*, in which he wrote:

Prayer is no panacea, no substitute for action. It is, rather, like a beam thrown from a flashlight before us into the darkness. It is in this light that we who grope, stumble, and climb, discover where we stand, what surrounds us, and the course which we should choose. Prayer makes visible the right, and reveals what is hampering and false. In its radiance, we behold the worth of our efforts, the range of our hopes, and the meaning of our deeds. Envy and fear, despair and resentment, anguish and grief, which lie heavily upon the heart, are dispelled like shadows by its light.

Although we must take responsibility for our health, we must also avoid blaming ourselves—or God—when disease strikes or recurs. One of the central truths I have tried to impart to my ailing parishioners is that illness is not a sign of inadequacy, pain is not a punishment. As we use the Psalms to pray for solace and recovery, we must know that disease is intrinsic to the human condition and that recovery is a gift, not a statement about our worthiness. The confused elitism that somehow those who heal their [bodies] are 'better' than those who don't has a tendency to come back as a sense of failure on the deathbed when the last disease inevitably comes along and displaces us naturally from the body," writes Levine in *Healing into Life and Death.* "Death is not a failure, but rather an event during the ongoing process which one survives on the path of healing to continue toward even greater learning and growth."

In *Healing Words*, Dr. Dossey uses irony to show why all of our specific prayers cannot be answered exactly as we wish them to be: "If all the prayers for curing disease that have been uttered in the history of the human race had been granted, almost no one would have died. This would have resulted in global disaster millennia ago through massive overpopulation. Today there would be no place to stand, and the Earth would be unfit for human habitation."

Dr. Dossey's comment is a humorous and sane prelude to a mature understanding of God. What is a mature faith? A perspective that allows us to see God as a compassionate Deity who has granted free will to human beings rather than one who has rigged the universe to reward the good with ceaseless health and immortality. Such a universe would be akin to an animal experiment in which we adopt moral behavior not because we have used our life journeys to discover intrinsic sources of love and empathy but because we expect physical well-being as a prize for good behavior.

Nor is God an authoritarian father figure who punishes with illness and death. I do not believe that God uses illness as a teaching tool. If illness and death were punishments, they would be visited exclusively upon the wicked. Yet terrible diseases are visited upon those who embody goodness as well as those who personify evil. There can be no humanity without illness and death. Indeed, *health* would have no meaning if there were not disease to hold up as a comparison. Rocks and robots will endure through the ages, but they cannot think, feel, create, or care for others. We can, and the price we pay for consciousness and free will is vulnerability and mortality.

But God does have one teaching instrument: the human conscience. We have an inborn mental reflex, one that causes emotional suffering and forces us to reflect on our actions when we behave badly. Another term for this suffering is *healthy guilt*, as opposed to unhealthy shame or gratuitous self-blame. This emotional reflex is God's way of implanting a moral compass in our hearts and minds.

The Psalms affirm a mature faith in their poetic evocations of a compassionate God, such as in Psalm 103:

> *The Lord executes righteous acts*
> *and judgments for all who are wronged.*
> *He made known His ways to Moses,*
> *His deeds to the children of Israel.*
> *The Lord is compassionate and gracious,*
> *slow to anger, abounding in steadfast love. . . .*
> *He has not dealt with us according to our sins,*
> *nor has He requited us according to our*
> *iniquities.*
> *For as the heavens are high above the earth,*
> *so great is His steadfast love toward those who*
> *fear Him.*

If God is compassionate, what can we ask of Him? What can we seek from the Psalms or any prayerful practice? Hope? Strength? Emotional healing? Spiritual connectedness? Physical recovery?

The answer, I believe, is all of the above, and it is perfectly legitimate to pray for our own recovery or for the recovery of a loved one. But to prevent shame and disillusion, it helps not only to hold lightly to expectation but also to focus our petitions on the real-world miracle workers who do God's work.

My teacher at the Jewish Theological Seminary in New York City, Robert Gordis, Ph.D., once wrote in his booklet *The Ladder of Prayer*, that when we pray for recovery, we might ask the Lord to release all of the forces in the universe that are required for healing. These are forces that exist, for example, within the doctors and nurses to whom we entrust our care. We might ask that our healers be empowered with all of their skills and intelligence as they implement the finest available medical treatments.

Yet we must also recognize that in the absence of physical recovery, we may still find a profound spiritual and emotional healing. Psalm 147 offers insight into healing

◆   ◆   ◆

beyond cure: "He heals their broken hearts, and binds up their wounds."

Responding to the question "How should I pray?" Dr. Dossey suggests that there is no correct answer. We must feel free to find our own uniquely personal approach to prayer. But he notes that there are two broad categories: directed prayer, in which we ask for a specific goal, image, or outcome, and nondirected or "open-ended" prayer, in which no specific outcome is held in the mind.

Theologians have long argued over the relative efficacy of directed and nondirected prayer, otherwise known as the "make it happen" and "let it be" approaches. Certainly, both forms of petition have validity. But one reason to consider the nondirected approach to prayer is that it acknowledges a higher intelligence: We don't always know precisely what is best for ourselves or our loved ones.

Nondirected prayer is humble prayer in which we simply ask for realization of the highest good. A perfect example is the open-hearted wisdom found in Psalm 31: "Into Your hand I entrust my spirit; You redeem me, O Lord, faithful God."

What We Need When We
Are Ill or Grieving

One beautiful aspect of the Book of Psalms is how it speaks truthfully to the human condition. When struggling with a life-threatening disease or dealing with a loved one who is gravely ill, most of us go through periods of anger, anxiety, and sadness as well as periods of exultation, relief, acceptance, insight, and joy. There will be times when we are full of fight and other times when we are overcome by exhaustion and hopelessness. The Psalms mirror these shifting states. From one Psalm or even one passage to the next, the Psalmist may turn to God in utter helplessness, frank despair, angry pleading, wistful entreaty, or joyous celebration.

Thus, the Psalms validate our shifting shades of experience when we are seriously ill or grieving. Modern-day psychologists and clergy who work with the sick and dying accept this range of emotion. They recognize, as we all should, that this entire spectrum is normal, that the only way out of feelings of rage, anxiety, or despair is to acknowledge and express them. We get stuck in painful emotions when we use denial to shunt them from consciousness or when we dwell on them because we have not fully worked through them. We can look to different Psalms to authenticate our experience at any particular juncture in our struggle with illness:

Have mercy on me, O Lord, for I languish;
*   heal me, O Lord, for my bones shake with terror.*
*   (Psalm 6:3)*

I say to God, my rock,
*   "Why have You forgotten me,*
*   why must I walk in gloom,*
*   oppressed by my enemy?". . .*
Why so downcast, my soul,
*   why disquieted within me?*
*   (Psalm 42:10, 12)*

You turned my lament into dancing,
*   You undid my sackcloth and girded me with joy,*
*   that [my] whole being might sing hymns to You*
*   endlessly;*
O Lord my God, I will praise You forever.
*   (Psalm 30:12-13)*

My deep distress increases;
deliver me from my straits.
Look at my affliction and suffering,
and forgive all my sins.

(PSALM 25:17-18)

My heart is firm, O God;
I will sing and chant a hymn with all my soul.
Awake, O harp and lyre!
I will wake the dawn.

(PSALM 108:2-3)

One of the most perplexing and difficult aspects of illness is the roller coaster ride between fighting spirit and hopeless resignation. Although we can try to maintain fighting spirit, it is generally impossible to stay relentlessly positive. In fact, trying to do so can be both exhausting and painful, especially if we work overtime to sustain a cheerful facade for friends and family. It is best to accept these shifts, referred to by cancer psychotherapist Robert Chernin Cantor, author of *And a Time to Live*, as the "resistance-surrender cycle." But how we give in to fatigue and helplessness is critical. Do we take time out for solitude and reflection, or do we isolate ourselves? Do we share our distress or keep it strictly to ourselves? Do we rest and meditate or languish in front of the television? Do we adopt a nihilistic attitude or turn to spiritual practice for meaning and comfort? Periods of "surrender" can be sources of regeneration if we accept them as part of the illness experience rather than prisons of despair from which we will never emerge.

The Psalms offer help whether we find ourselves in the resistance or surrender phase of the coping cycle. *For Thou Art with Me* offers Psalms of celebration and thanksgiving, which can suit us perfectly when our fighting spirit is high. And it offers Psalms full of anguish and entreaties for help, which are helpful when our energy is down and our spirits are depleted.

Jon Kabat-Zinn, Ph.D., head of the stress reduction clinic at the University of Massachusetts Medical School in Worcester, treats patients with chronic diseases who remain sick despite every conceivable medical therapy. Dr. Kabat-Zinn teaches them mindfulness meditation, a Buddhist contemplative practice in which the focus is on breathing and the present moment. The essence of mindfulness is learning to stay in the present. The meditator "watches" the flow of thoughts as they move in and out of consciousness; he or she returns again and again to the

breath and to an awareness of each moment. Joan Bory-
senko, Ph.D., a cell biologist and mind-body therapist in
Boulder, Colorado, once commented that mindfulness is
really a form of gratitude. When we pay attention to the
moment, we inevitably appreciate our gifts: the extraordinary pleasures of the five senses, the magnificence of the
natural world, the transcendent joy of being with people
we love—our spouses, children, parents, and friends.

Many Psalms are themselves mindfulness meditations, as
they extol the treasures of the natural world, the wonders
of the human body, or the omnipresence of a compassionate power greater than ourselves. Psalms of gratitude
are odes to the moment, grounding us in the present,
training our focus on what we have rather than what we
lack. When we praise God through the Psalms, or through
daily blessings from our own religious liturgies, we pay
homage to the grand possibilities of the moment, in spite
of our suffering.

What do we need when sick or grieving? The love and
support of friends and family. Respect for our uniquely
personal coping process, including our emotional highs and
lows. Mindfulness in the sense of gratitude—the strength
not only to mourn our losses but also to embrace the gifts
of the moment. The skillful care of medical professionals

empowered to fulfill their charge as healers. Deep sources of spiritual sustenance in the form of prayer or other rituals of worship to a God of kindness and love. In this book, we offer selections from the Psalms that help to meet these needs. We will deliver the Psalms in a concise, excerpted form designed to inspire the sick and the suffering.

Our book offers 15 of the Psalms with our commentaries. Each Psalm addresses an aspect of the suffering associated with illness, or meets a particular emotional or spiritual yearning on the part of patients or families. Thus, to guide you toward Psalms that will help at a particular time, we've given each chapter (one Psalm and its commentary) a title referring to the need it meets. For instance, the title for the chapter on Psalm 31 is "To Ease Shame and Sorrow."

For Thou Art with Me will serve patients and their families as a kind of handbook for the soul. But rather than relying on a contemporary language of self-help, the book will offer the ancient language of the most celebrated biblical poetry, words that have lifted the spirits of people for 3,000 years. "Surely goodness and mercy shall follow me all the days of my life: and I will dwell in the house of the Lord forever."

What other words ring with such hope and glory through the ages?

PSALM 6

◆ ◆ ◆

TO RECEIVE OUR PRAYERS
FOR HEALING

The Lord heeds my plea,

the Lord accepts my prayer.

To Receive Our Prayers for Healing

Psalm 6

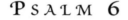

. . . Have mercy on me, O Lord, for I languish;
  heal me, O Lord, for my bones shake with terror.
My whole being is stricken with terror,
  while You, Lord—O, how long!
O Lord, turn! Rescue me!
Deliver me as befits Your faithfulness.
For there is no praise of You among the dead;
  in Sheol [the netherworld], who can acclaim You?

I am weary with groaning;
  every night I drench my bed,
  I melt my couch in tears.
My eyes are wasted by vexation,
  worn out because of all my foes.
Away from me, all you evildoers,
  for the Lord heeds the sound of my weeping.
The Lord heeds my plea,
  the Lord accepts my prayer. . . .

A poem by and for the afflicted, Psalm 6 speaks to the sheer fright and anguish that can accompany a severe illness. The Psalmist's "bones shake with terror," as does his "whole being," or in other translations, his "soul." Our spirit suffers along with our flesh as we wrestle with anxiety, sadness, even despair. These feelings become intertwined with our physical pains, reinforcing one another across the channels that connect mind and body.

When we are stricken with disease of body and mind, we plead for healing: "Heal me, O Lord. . . . " We can turn to the God of our understanding whenever we're caught in the spiritual, emotional, and physical grip of ill health.

Cosmic loneliness worsens physical suffering, and the afflicted one reaches out to God for help, sustenance, and the return of wellness. "Deliver me as befits Your faithfulness." The root of the Hebrew word for *faithfulness* is closest to *love*. God's love will bring us home to healing, whether of body, soul, or both. Those of us languishing with illness can be assured that a God of love wants us to get well, that our continuing illness is not a divine punishment but part of our intrinsic human condition. God wants us well, and our prayers are heard and heeded, though not always in the form of complete physical recovery. God does not respond to our prayers the way a first-class mail-order company faithfully delivers its products. Being heard by God, though, cures our spiritual isolation. That is itself a profound form of healing beyond biological recovery. Psalm 6 is a cry for being heard.

"For there is no praise of You among the dead," a neatly ironic turn of phrase, is the Psalmist's plea for life. The Psalms originated before certain strands of Jewish theology developed their own unique concept of the soul's immortality. Whether we accept or reject the notion of an afterlife, the great religious and spiritual traditions embrace the sanctity of *this* life, the imperative that we try to hold on to our loved ones, our work, our conscious intellectual and spiritual life. This philosophy can be found here and elsewhere in the Psalms.

This Psalm's poetic expression of physical and spiritual suffering is suffused with painfully familiar images. "Every night I drench my bed" conjures the night sweats of severe infection, AIDS, or the adverse effects of treatment with chemotherapy. "My eyes are wasted by vexation, worn out because of all my foes" indicates that the sufferer is at wit's end, his eyes are weary and, as one interpreter says, "his sight fails as in a man of advanced age."

Have you ever been so ill and frightened that your body is soaked with sweat and your bed with tears? In your dread and loneliness, the Psalm implies, you have God's company, His omnipresent empathy.

But who are the "foes" who cause the Psalmist's misery? Enemies abound in the Psalms, and we rarely know exactly who they are. I once spoke to an academic whose seminary thesis was an attempt to uncover the identity of the enemies that appear in the Psalms like the scores of secondary cast members in a big adventure film. She abandoned the effort after several seemingly futile years of research. So perhaps we should understand these references in the Psalms as metaphors and locate their deeper meanings. (We would do this with any other form of poetry.)

Psalm 6 is so clearly about illness, and the "foes" and "evildoers" the Psalmist wishes to banish can be viewed as agents of disease. The ancients knew nothing of viruses, bacteria, environmental pollutants, and cancer cells, but their language implies a sense of malevolent forces out to get us when we're bedded down with sickness. Those of us who are sick can easily understand these allusions to enemies if we perceive them as microscopic pathogens—the invisible interlopers that actually cause most of our maladies. Once we do, we can hope and pray and take medicines to help us conquer the foes within. "Away from me, all you evildoers, for the Lord heeds the sound of my weeping."

Yes, the Lord not only hears but *heeds* the sound of our weeping, and we can turn to God in His beneficence for the strength we need in our own biological battles against microbial adversaries. Some of us want strength for what we perceive as a fight. Others pray for the strength to simply accept cohabitation with pathogens of all kinds, gently encouraging the immune system to maintain a peaceful détente. We should respect our own unique personal tendencies as we pray for whatever kind of strength we feel is regenerative.

What if we give up and become hopeless? God will not punish us because we are spiritually and physically depleted. But hopelessness can itself be an illness, not one of weakness but of psychic vulnerability. If we find ourselves constantly hopeless, especially early in the course of an illness, we can—indeed, we should—turn to our families, friends, and God for help.

A recent study of breast cancer patients confirmed what older studies suggested: Chronic hopelessness is itself a kind of pathogen; patients who felt utter despair were more likely to have progressive disease. So, we can counter hopelessness just as we would counter the invading bug—with conviction, ingenuity, and a willingness to procure help. (How many of us stricken by infection would refuse to go to a doctor for medication and tending?) Not only loved ones but also therapists, psychiatrists, and pastoral counselors can be sources of love and support. We may need to make an inner journey to root out the various causes of our despair so that we can reclaim our desire for life.

I will never forget the time, years ago, when I received a phone call at 2:00 A.M. The family of a member of my congregation, Walter, wanted me to join them by his hospital bedside. Walter had been stricken with a terrible bleeding ulcer, and despite the ministrations of his doctor, he was on the verge of death. I sat with Walter, held his hand as he hallucinated, and remained with him in the hour before he passed away. I spent early-morning hours comforting the family members, and afterward, Walter's physician, Jack, asked if I would speak with him. Jack was not only Walter's doctor, he was also a longtime dear friend of his.

"Rabbi, he shouldn't have died," said Jack, with evident pain in his voice. "We can save people with bleeding ulcers, and I told him that he was going to be okay. But Walter came into the hospital, saying over and over, 'I'm going to die.' I argued with him, insisting that he would recover and that I would take care of him. He did not seem to hear me at all, he was so convinced that his demise was inevitable." Jack, the soul of a compassionate physician, broke down and cried. Together, we grieved over the man we knew, the man who should not have died.

Walter had no hope, and his prophecy seemed self-fulfilling. Many of us know or have heard stories of people who died swiftly following a collapse into resignation. Our experience—and even some research—suggests that the link here is real.

We must never judge those who, like Walter, lose hope, for we often know too little of what it means to be inside their skins. We rarely understand the forces that push people over an abyss into despair. We can only care for these people in life and in death, as Jack did. But we must know, too, that our care means doing whatever we can to ease their despair.

If we happen to be the sick ones feeling despair, we must not judge ourselves. Nor should we be mortified by our own feelings. But we can try to muster the courage to ask for help, since human contact—the knowledge, warmth, and love of family and caring professionals—can help us exit the trap of chronic hopelessness. So can spiritual contact, through ritual, prayer, or turning to a Psalm such as this one.

The voice in Psalm 6 is battling hopelessness, and he or she is winning the battle. The Psalmist's entreaties to God are a cry for breath, for sustenance, for life. The mere cry itself is a sign of life, and in the end, the Psalmist's petition is heard. "The Lord heeds my plea, the Lord accepts my prayer."

A while ago, I met a woman, Susan, at a gathering of close friends. Susan was contending with a serious cancer, and she was undergoing an arduous experimental drug regimen. She was receiving medical and emotional help in her struggle, but some friends were being solicitous in a way that implied, "Oh, poor you." Susan resisted that kind of help and its meaning. "Don't pity me, because I'm not deterred by any of this," was her message.

Susan was determined to live her life as always. She had children in different parts of the country, and she visited them often—regularly traveling, for instance, from Boston to California. She had to fly back home after each visit for her drug treatments. She would typically complete her next round of therapy and get right back on a plane to see her children and grandchildren again. The visits were pure tonics, offsetting the negative drug effects as surely as analgesics or antiemetics. Back at home, Susan spent much of her time on the phone with her travel agent.

"I will never give up," she said. "I'll go on living as normally as possible and fighting this disease as long as I can." Susan's belief was clear: The notion that it was God's will that she be sick or remain sick was bogus. "God wants me to continue to fight the good fight and to get well," she said. Susan was enlivened by the mere idea that God was in her corner. Somehow, this never led her to view God as a mythic savior, guaranteed to wrest her from disease, but rather as the very source of her fortitude. As far as I know, Susan's hope and determination helped her to live for a long time, though I have since lost touch with her.

Susan's story makes me think about the most important line in Psalm 6, "the Lord accepts my prayer." The Lord does not answer our prayers with instant recovery as much as He accepts our prayers. When we honor life and turn to others and to God, we receive Divine *acceptance*, a healing beyond our fleshly status, beyond life and death.

PSALM 23

◆ ◆ ◆

TO RESTORE OUR SOULS

Yea, though I walk through the valley

of the shadow of death,

I will fear no evil:

for Thou art with me...

To Restore Our Souls

Psalm 23

◆ ◆ ◆

The Lord is my shepherd;
I shall not want.
He makes me lie down in green pastures;
He leads me beside the still waters.
He restores my soul;
He leads me in the paths of righteousness
for His name's sake.

Yea, though I walk through the valley of the
shadow of death,
I will fear no evil: for Thou art with me;
Thy rod and Thy staff, they comfort me.

Thou preparest a meal before me in the presence
of my enemies;
Thou anointest my head with oil;
my cup runs over.
Surely goodness and mercy shall follow me
all the days of my life,
and I will dwell in the house of the
Lord forever.

Undoubtedly the most revered of all the Psalms, Psalm 23 is embraced by people of varied faiths, and especially by Jews and Christians of all denominations, who rely on its exquisitely comforting words in times of grief and crisis. The Psalm is often spoken or sung at funerals, and while it is the single most consoling poem for the bereaved, it may also be the most sustaining poem for people who are afflicted with illness and for the loved ones who stand by their sides.

The first three verses present God as the ground of all creation: He gives us nature, He gives us peace, He restores our souls. Then comes the verse that has fired the spiritual imagination of generations: "Yea, though I walk through the valley of the shadow of death, I will fear no evil: for Thou art with me; Thy rod and Thy staff, they comfort me."

The reference to the valley of the shadow of death explains the Psalm's use during times of grief, but it also helps explain its inestimable value to people in the midst of mortal struggle. The Psalmist does not walk *into* the valley of the shadow of death, he walks *through* it. The bereaved individual has been engulfed in the shadow of the death of his loved one, and he endures. He moves through his grief. Likewise, the person dealing with life-threatening illness finds himself in the valley, but Psalm 23 will have him walk *through* it—moving through pain and struggle, coming out the other side, without fear. What is the other side? Is it life or death? Either way, God never ultimately abandons us: ". . . and I will dwell in the house of the Lord forever." Our souls, the ones "He restores," are indeed immortal.

"I will fear no evil: for Thou art with me" crystallizes the meaning and the message that are at the heart of the entire Book of Psalms. No human being, no animal, no natural disaster, and no disease—no matter how malevolent or destructive—can rip apart our souls, because they are forever safeguarded by an eternally loving God. The purpose of prayer and of turning to the Psalms is not merely to remind ourselves of this eternal truth but to *live* this truth.

In discussing the power of Psalm 23, Rabbi Harold Kushner makes a telling observation about its construction. In his book *Who Needs God*, Rabbi Kushner notes that in the first several verses, when the Psalm describes how God is present in times of peace and normalcy, the Psalmist talks *about* God: "He makes me lie down in green pastures." "But when things go badly," writes Rabbi Kushner, "when we find ourselves walking in the valley of the shadow of death, that is when God becomes real. No longer an abstract 'He,' God is now 'Thou': 'I could never have made it through this time were it not for You.'"

When we're going through that valley ourselves, that is when God shifts in our minds and hearts from "He" to "Thou." A dear friend and former member of my Boston-area congregation, Edwin Kolodny, M.D., experienced this transformation in his own time of crisis. Ed, a distinguished physician who specializes in genetic diseases of the nervous system, has since moved to New York, where he is now professor and chairman of the department of neurology at New York University Medical Center in New York City.

Five years ago, he was diagnosed with serious heart disease and set to undergo heart bypass surgery. Ed was gripped by fear as he was wheeled on a stretcher into a narrow hospital corridor, where he awaited entry to the operating room. He later wrote me a letter about his experience, including this description of events leading up to his surgery:

The dreaded moment comes, a stranger brings by a hard litter, you summon up your remaining energies to "move over" and off you go with a well-meaning pat from the ward nurse who tucks your chart under the mattress with the parting words "good luck." Neither these nor any other well-meaning gestures could prepare even the hospital-savvy physician for the world of klieg lights, white-tiled operating amphitheater, machines, instruments, monitors, tubes, and poles of every description with innumerable blue-capped and gowned and masked fellow human beings . . . nurses, doctors, and technicians moving helter-skelter in patterns familiar only to them, and their colleagues with whom they daily share life and death. . . .

The entryway to the operating room area . . . is a bank of five elevators. Being a "first case" on the schedule for my surgeon, my stretcher entered this narrow, congested corridor at about the same time as four or five other patients on stretchers. With room for only one stretcher at a time to pass and with dozens of blue-robed people moving about this narrow passageway, one disruption to the flow of traffic could have paralyzed the entire hospital.

The doctor is now a patient, and his world has gone topsy-turvy. His sense of helplessness is palpable in his description of life on the stretcher. Then comes the turning point in Ed's story, and I will let his words capture it:

Then a miracle happened, and a lifetime of devotion to Judaism bestowed on me a reward that is almost impossible to describe. . . .

At that moment, I spotted a middle-aged woman holding a Book of Psalms. [She was the wife of another surgical patient.] With the greatest challenge of my action-packed life before me, I reached my arm out to her and said, "Say a blessing for me." Mrs. G., my angel, steps right into the middle of this incredibly congested corridor, stopping *everything*. And held open her text to the 23rd Psalm, and with everything at a complete standstill—elevators, machines, technicians, litter bearers—prompting me along, my voice hesitating at points, [as] I said, "The Lord is my Shepherd; I shall not want . . ." until the end of the Psalm. When I finished, the frenetic pace of the operating room resumed.

During my recitation, however, no one moved—even though I was just another anonymous patient. But finally, I was ready! I could face anything. The O.R. machines, tubes, masked faces, could do what they had to. I was set!

A few days later, Mrs. G. stopped by to visit me and to report that her husband's relatively minor colon operation had gone well. I am not a particularly emotional person (except inside), but I still cannot contain my tears when I think of that moment, the greatest challenge of my life, when God appeared and gave me fortitude and peace that nothing until then had achieved.

For Ed, God was no longer an abstraction but a living reality, personified by Mrs. G., manifest in the transcendent language of the 23rd Psalm. With the now lucid belief that God was with him, he was able to brook any fear, and he entered the surgical suite in a state of preternatural calm. He was unconscious under anesthesia for hours while his heart was stopped and repaired, but long after his recovery, he held fast to the memory of Mrs. G. and his reading of the Psalm, and his faith was forever strengthened.

One of the glories of Psalm 23 is that it speaks to all of us, whether we are sick, in crisis, or concerned about a loved one. And it speaks to us wherever we are on the continuum of coping: in the stage of anger, dread, depression, acceptance, grief, or gratitude. In all these circumstances, "He leads [us] in the paths of righteousness for His name's sake." The final verse suggests that God is with us in life and beyond the physical and temporal borders of life. "Surely goodness and mercy shall follow me all the days of my life, and I will dwell in the house of the Lord forever." For those of us facing the prospect of death after an illness, it is only fitting that *forever* is the Psalm's last word. Yes, our suffering will end, but we will not be not released into an abyss. We will be released into the house of the Lord.

Yet I have found Psalm 23 particularly comforting for patients dealing with an equivocal prognosis, such as the cancer patient who is told that she has a 50-50 chance of full recovery. While I have trouble with the book-maker's approach to life-and-death situations, every such patient—no matter how tactfully her doctors frame her condition—knows that she is in a struggle for life. Unless she uses denial as a way to cope, she is bound to feel some terror, some bewilderment, and a heavy burden of stress as she undergoes medical treatment with no guar-antee of cure.

"For Thou art with me" may be a mantra for any of us when we are dispossessed of our normal lives by illness, thrust into a regimen of difficult therapies, unable to es-cape the global truth that "healthy" people can more blithely disregard: that we are all mortal and time is short. Life is precious, so death, whether it seems impending or far away, is not something that we ought to deflect with a shrug of denial. We can only confront the loss of life—our own or our loved ones'—with grief, lest we cut ourselves off from the very humanity that makes our lives so worth living. But we can still be profoundly comforted by the knowledge of something more beyond death. Here is how Rabbi Kushner expresses it in *Who Needs God*:

My religious experience offers me the assurance that, though my body will one day give out, the essential Me will live on, and if I am concerned with immortality of that sort, I should pay at least as much attention to my soul, my non-physical self, as I do my weight and my blood pressure. God cannot redeem me from death, no matter how good a person I am, but He redeems me from the fear of death so that I don't have to clutch frantically at this life as if it were all there is. He lights my path through the "valley of the shadow of death" by assuring me that the words I have written and spoken, the hearts I have touched, the hands I have reached out to, the child I will leave behind, will gain me all the immortality I need. More than that, I am assured that even when the last person who ever knew me dies, and the last copy of my book has been removed from the library shelf, the essential me, the nonphysical me, will still live on in the mind of God, where no act of goodness or kindness is ever forgotten.

Rabbi Kushner is pointing out that an essential part of who we are—*the* essential part—is one with God. When we shuffle off this mortal coil, we are no more or less united with God. During this life and whatever awaits us afterward, we dwell perpetually in the house of the Lord. With this transcendent idea at its core, Psalm 23 extends its succor to all suffering beings, throughout eternity.

PSALM 30

◆ ◆ ◆

TO FIND OUR WAY BACK
TO WELLNESS

Weeping may linger for the night;

but joy comes

in the morning.

To Find Our Way Back
to Wellness

PSALM 30

♦ ♦ ♦

I extol You, O Lord,
  for You have lifted me up,
  and not let my enemies rejoice over me.
O Lord, my God,
  I cried out to You,
  and You healed me.
O Lord, You brought me up from Sheol [the
    netherworld],
  preserved me from going down into the Pit.

O you faithful of the Lord, sing to Him,
  and praise His holy name.
For He is angry but a moment,
  and when He is pleased there is life.
Weeping may linger for the night;
  but at dawn there are shouts of joy.

When I was untroubled,
  I thought, "I shall never be shaken,"
  for You, O Lord, when You were pleased,
  made [me] firm as a mighty mountain.
When You hid Your face,
  I was terrified.
I called to You, O Lord;
  to my Lord I made appeal,
  "What is to be gained from my death,
  from my descent into the Pit?
Can dust praise You?
Can it declare Your faithfulness?
Hear, O Lord, and have mercy on me;
  O Lord, be my help!"

You turned my lament into dancing,
  You undid my sackcloth and girded me with joy,
  that [my] whole being might sing hymns to
    You endlessly;
  O Lord my God, I will praise You forever.

This Psalm is one I recommend most often to those who are sick or in crisis, for it can bring courage and strength in times of dire distress. The entire Psalm follows the arc of recovery, from fear and suffering to eventual healing, through a transformative experience of faith and, ultimately, gratitude. Indeed, the Psalmist appears to be someone who has recovered from serious illness and offers the Psalm as thanksgiving.

I often suggest to people in the midst of crisis that they recall the traditional translation of verse 6: "Weeping may linger for the night, but joy comes in the morning." It suggests that faith can sustain us through anguish and bring us through darkness into a new morning, when "a ringing cry of joy" (literal translation) reverberates in our hearts and minds. In another translation, weeping "comes to lodge in the evening." The Reverend Dr. A. Cohen, general editor of the *Soncino Books of the Bible*, writes that weeping is thus "likened to a passing traveller who arrives at dusk to spend the night in a place of shelter and proceeds on his way in the morning."

The image of weeping as a passing traveller helps us to recognize that our suffering is transitory, that joy will be possible in the morning—if not the next morning, then soon again on another morning. It reminds us that the rhythms of emotional and physical healing are cyclical, that pain need not become an endless trap, especially when we find strength through a prayerful expression of faith.

In the spring of 1977, I was in a typical work crunch—preparing for the festival of Shavuot, writing sermons, getting ready for our Hebrew school graduation—when I received a frantic phone call from a congregant informing me that one of our members, Leah, had suffered a serious heart attack and was not expected to live. Only in her midthirties, Leah was unable to speak when I visited her in the hospital. I said a prayer for her and tried to comfort her husband and two young children. That same evening, I received a call from Leah's husband saying that she had died. He requested that I come immediately to their house to comfort Leah's mother, who was hysterical and crying inconsolably.

The scene at Leah's house was unutterably sad. Leah's mother, Sarah, railed bitterly against a God who would take her daughter at such a young age. "How could God be so cruel and unfair?" she demanded of me. I sat down with her and tried to explain that Leah's death was not a result of God's cruelty; it may have had genetic or congenital origins. God did not control every facet of our fate, I said, but He did want us to find the strength to face this great loss. In time, Sarah calmed down, and I returned to my home.

Although I do not believe that the stress of Leah's death and my encounter with her bereaved mother was the sole cause of what subsequently happened to me, the tragedy may well have been a trigger. That same evening, I developed severe chest pains and was rushed to the hospital, where I was diagnosed as having had a heart attack. It was not immediately clear what this attack would portend for my future. Would I fully recover, or would I be plagued with heart disease for years? The crisis passed and I was discharged, but in the days that followed, I was beset by fears that I would become an invalid, that I might never be able to fully return to my rabbinical work, which, along with my family, gave my life purpose and joy. I found myself turning, for the first time, to that verse in Psalm 30: "Weeping may linger for the night, but joy comes in the morning." Whenever I felt overcome by despair, I would recite the verse to myself. It had a nearly magical effect, easing my fears and restoring my hope. I eventually was able to return to work full-time, learning to pace myself better and care for my health.

Every single day since the spring of 1977, I have turned to Psalm 30 as part of my daily prayer ritual. I always pause as I say to myself, "Weeping may linger for the night, but joy comes in the morning." When I required triple bypass surgery several years ago, I turned again to this verse of faith and regeneration, and it remains a precious companion.

For many serious illnesses, the recovery process can be protracted, the inevitable setbacks and small triumphs accompanied by extreme vicissitudes of emotion. But Psalm 30 lightens the heart with the eventual possibility of convalescence and a return to health and the fullness of life. "You turned my lament into dancing, You undid my sackcloth and girded me with joy."

The transformative arc that is apparent in Psalm 30 reminds us of the healing potential of faith. "I cried out to You, and You healed me" crystallizes the message, but the Psalmist—who stands for all of us—did not always turn to God. "When I was untroubled, I thought, 'I shall never be shaken.'" When all is well, we take divine grace for granted. "When You hid Your face, I was terrified." During illness, impending surgery, loss, or emotional crisis, we may feel that we have lost our connection to God, and our terror deepens.

But prayer restores communication with the Almighty, as the Psalmist makes a passionate appeal to God for His understanding and mercy: "What is to be gained from my death?" "Can dust praise You?" "O Lord, be my help!"

The Psalm's denouement teaches that our prayers can be heard, turning our laments into dancing, freeing us of our sackcloths, and girding us with joy. This allows our whole being to sing hymns endlessly, to praise God forever. Restoring communication with the Divine by asking for help and offering praise represents our passage through that dark night of the soul that so often characterizes our confrontations with illness or death.

Psalm 30 reminds us of a paradox that often occurs among those of us stricken with life-threatening illness. I have been told by some patients with cancer and heart disease that their illnesses have been great "teachings." A few have even remarked that their brushes with mortality have been "the best thing that ever happened." What explains such a strange eventuality? Who among us would suspect that we would be grateful for *any* aspect of a grave illness?

Renowned psychotherapist Lawrence LeShan, Ph.D., has reported scores of cases in which patients experienced cancer as a positive "turning point." Psalm 30 recalls the moment of such a turn, when the Psalmist called to God and "made appeal." The return to faith, regardless of its form, can yield both the strength to recover and the recognition of our vast potential for joyous living—in the present moment, as the Buddhists would say, with gratitude and exaltation.

Psalm 30 reveals that the return to spiritual connectedness prompted by an illness can indeed be a gift to the patient and his or her family. The anguish of sickness is no less real and no less regrettable. But the recognition that joy comes in the morning brings not only renewed faith but a sweetness to all our remaining days, regardless of their number. It also brings awareness that pain and fear are often transient, while our true spiritual nature is both timeless and boundless.

PSALM 32

◆ ◆ ◆

TO HEAL THROUGH
CONFESSION

You are my shelter;

You preserve me

from distress;

You surround me with the joyous shouts

of deliverance.

TO HEAL THROUGH CONFESSION

PSALM 32

———◆———◆———◆———

Happy is he whose transgression is forgiven,
  whose sin is covered over.
Happy the man whom the Lord does not hold guilty,
  and in whose spirit there is no deceit.

As long as I said nothing,
  my limbs wasted away
  from my anguished roaring all day long.
For night and day
  Your hand lay heavy on me;
  my vigor waned
  as in the summer drought.
Then I acknowledged my sin to You;
  I did not cover up my guilt;
  I resolved, "I will confess my transgressions to
    the Lord,"
  and You forgave the guilt of my sin.

Therefore let every faithful man pray to You
  upon discovering [his sin],
  that the rushing mighty waters
  not overtake him.
You are my shelter;
  You preserve me from distress;
  You surround me with the joyous shouts of
    deliverance.

Let me enlighten you
  and show you which way to go;
  let me offer counsel; my eye is on you.
Be not like a senseless horse or mule
  whose movement must be curbed by bit and bridle;
  far be it from you!
Many are the torments of the wicked,
  but he who trusts in the Lord
  shall be surrounded with favor.
Rejoice in the Lord and exult, O you righteous;
  shout for joy, all upright men!

Whether we are ill, dealing with the illness of a loved one, or grieving a loss, the burden of guilt can intensify our suffering. Sometimes, the mind-body scientists tell us, we can even become sick if we harbor profound guilt over a real or imagined transgression, guilt that we can never relieve because we remain forever silent about our feelings.

Psalm 32 is a powerful expression of the transformation of guilt through confession and God's forgiveness. Confiding the truth to ourselves and to God, we find both resolution and a divine form of absolution.

Guilt certainly has its place in the repertoire of human emotions; it is the expression of a wounded conscience. When we harm someone with our words, we ought to feel guilty. When we destroy someone's reputation with our gossip, we ought to feel guilty. When we abuse our spouse or children or parents, we ought to feel guilty. Healthy guilt is a vital message from within, from the part of ourselves capable of authentic compassion, and from without, the collective moral code of society bringing its weight to bear on our consciousness.

But many of us are subject to unhealthy guilt, which is excessive or wholly unjustified. I often recognize unhealthy guilt in people with serious illness who somehow blame themselves for their misfortune. I also see unhealthy guilt in people who have lost a loved one. The surviving spouse will make comments such as, "Why didn't I recognize her illness sooner?" "Why did I leave the hospital to go home just before he died?" "Why did we have that bitter fight just before she became so sick?"

We torture ourselves with such questions, and as long as we

continue to feel guilty, we cannot rid ourselves of the crushing burden of grief. In fact, grief over our own illnesses or over the loss of a loved one is almost universally accompanied by guilt. Most often, such guilt is of the unhealthy variety, since there is no sound moral basis for our beliefs. Although some illnesses may be due to poor lifestyle habits or stress, we never wittingly make ourselves sick. Many of the most devoted and loving spouses, parents, and children still punish themselves with guilt over the loss of their loved ones.

Guilt is harmful when we remain mute in our suffering, compounding the pain by locking it up inside. Put simply, repressed guilt can make our lives miserable. "As long as I said nothing, my limbs wasted away from my anguished roaring all day long." Indeed, repressed guilt can sap our energies and perhaps even make us ill. "For night and day Your hand lay heavy on me; my vigor waned as in the summer drought."

Psalm 32 teaches that we heal guilt by confiding our anguish to someone who can listen and empathize—a counselor, clergyperson, therapist, or friend. And prayer can be a vehicle for confiding our anguish to God. The turning point in Psalm 32 is the moment of confession: "Then I acknowledged my sin to You; I did not cover up my guilt; I resolved, 'I will confess my transgressions to the Lord,' and You forgave the guilt of my sin."

The cleansing notion of confession is a feature of many faiths. We know that through confession, we relieve ourselves of unhealthy guilt and find our way toward spiritual revitalization. But even science has shown us the healing potential of confession. In a series of studies conducted by psychologist James Pennebaker, Ph.D., of Southern Methodist University in Dallas, people in a test group spent 30 minutes a day for 5 days writing out their deepest thoughts and feelings about traumatic, painful, or disturbing events of the past or present. For 5 months afterward, the people who "confided" these thoughts and feelings were both emotionally and physically healthier than the control group, who wrote about trivial subjects. Not only did the test group suffer fewer illnesses, but their immune cells, which defend against disease agents in the body, were also livelier and more responsive than before.

Dr. Pennebaker has repeated the study many times, and each time he has confirmed the healing power of confession. Importantly, the first stage of confession is acknowledging to ourselves our guilt, anger, fear, or sadness. Only then can we confide in another, overcoming our isolation and healing the loneliness that attends severe guilt.

When we confide to ourselves, we may also confide to God. "Happy the man whom the Lord does not hold guilty, and in whose spirit there is no deceit." The deceit ends when we fully confront our guilt and the underlying sorrow, healing the split within us and finding our way back to God. If the guilt is justified, we can find forgiveness by acknowledging our sin to ourselves and to our God. If the guilt is unjustified, we can be relieved of the undue burden by recognizing the deeper truth of our innocence, in our own eyes and the eyes of God.

In Dr. Pennebaker's studies, the subjects later reported that they felt not only relief but also resolution, a sense of peace regarding the trauma or transgression they had confided. Psalm 32 captures the return to harmony and joy in the aftermath of confession: "You surround me with the joyous shouts of deliverance." Those who turn to the Lord "shall be surrounded with favor."

For those of us who are sick or whose loved ones suffer with illness, releasing ourselves from the grip of unhealthy guilt is essential to healing. In our own eyes and the eyes of our God, we can accept our weaknesses and vulnerabilities, acknowledge our true responsibilities, and also reject the punishing voices of undeserved guilt. We can be both forgiven for true transgressions and released from imagined misdeeds. "Happy is he whose transgression is forgiven, whose sin is covered over."

PSALM 139

◆ ◆ ◆

TO HONOR THE SPIRIT
IN THE BODY

I praise You,

for I am awesomely,

wondrously made;

Your work is wonderful;

I know it very well.

TO HONOR THE SPIRIT
IN THE BODY

PSALM 139

◆ ◆ ◆

O Lord, You have examined me and know me.
When I sit down or stand up You know it;
You discern my thoughts from afar.
You observe my walking and reclining,
and are familiar with all my ways.
There is not a word on my tongue
but that You, O Lord, know it well.
You hedge me before and behind;
You lay Your hand upon me.
It is beyond my knowledge;
it is a mystery; I cannot fathom it.
Where can I escape from Your spirit?
Where can I flee from Your presence?
If I ascend to heaven, You are there;
if I descend to Sheol [the netherworld], You
are there too.

If I take wing with the dawn
*   to come to rest on the western horizon,*
*   even there Your hand will be guiding me,*
*   Your right hand will be holding me fast.*
If I say, "Surely darkness will conceal me,
*   night will provide me with cover,"*
*   darkness is not dark for You;*
*   night is as light as day;*
*   darkness and light are the same.*
It was You who created my conscience;
*   You fashioned me in my mother's womb.*
I praise You,
*   for I am awesomely, wondrously made;*
*   Your work is wonderful;*
*   I know it very well.*
My frame was not concealed from You
*   when I was shaped in a hidden place,*
*   knit together in the recesses of the earth.*
Your eyes saw my unformed limbs;
*   they were all recorded in Your book;*
*   in due time they were formed,*
*   to the very last one of them.*
How weighty Your thoughts seem to me, O God,
*   how great their number!*
I count them—they exceed the grains of sand;
*   I end—but am still with You. . . .*

This meditation on God's omnipresence in the universe
comforts us with the knowledge that God is always with

us wherever we go. It brings to mind the wonderful title of Dr. Jon Kabat-Zinn's book on mindfulness, *Wherever You Go, There You Are.* Psalm 139 could be titled, "Wherever You Go, There Is God." As the Psalmist contemplates God's omnipresence, the focus moves to the miracle of the human body, how God the creator has wrought such an intricate vessel, one that is "awesomely, wondrously made," reminding us that our healing potential is boundless.

Nowhere else in the Book of Psalms is God's omnipresence more purely expressed. In Psalm 139's early verses, God knows our every word and thought, He is "familiar with all [our] ways." Taken one way, the Psalmist may seem overwhelmed by God's pervasiveness in his life: "Where can I escape from Your spirit? Where can I flee from Your presence?" Yet God is no Big Brother in the Orwellian sense, for no matter where we go—"If I take wing with the dawn to come to rest on the western horizon"— He is present with loving support: "Even there Your hand will be guiding me."

God is omnipresent not as a harsh judge, as some biblical interpreters would have us accept. He sees and knows all with absolute compassion; He is everywhere a healing presence. This is no more perfectly captured than in the verse "You hedge me before and behind; You lay Your hand upon me." God protects us from the front and back; He surrounds us; but any paranoid view of his omnipresence is dispelled. The phrase used to describe the action of healers who use touch with loving intent is *the laying on of hands*. In Psalm 139, God *lays His hand* upon the Psalmist, gently caring for him. Like the Psalmist, we are indeed touched by God, a source of solace for those of us who feel wounded and alone with illness or grief.

The early images and ideas in Psalm 139 allow those of us saddled with illness to know that we are not isolated in a corner of the universe where God cannot see us, hear our petitions, envelop us in His loving awareness. When in the throes of illness or despair, late at night in a hospital room or late at night in bed, unable to sleep, we may feel an unutterable loneliness. Our prognoses may be uncertain, and we toss and turn, unable to escape the grasp of our worst fears. But "darkness is not dark for You; night is as light as day." We do not slip away from God, and God does not slip away from us, in those dark hours of gut-churning anxiety.

We then learn how God, not only all-present but also all-creative, designed our human bodies from the moment when the first microscopic specks of our material being came into existence. "You fashioned me in my mother's womb." In an older translation, the line "It was You who created my conscience" was "For Thou hast made my reins." *Reins* refers to the kidneys, which medical philosophers of antiquity believed to be the seat of the conscience. (For thousands of years, Chinese medicine has identified organs such as the kidneys as energy centers for functions of not just the body but also the mind.) God has created the body-mind complex from the ground up, from the time when we were "shaped in a hidden place, knit together in the recesses of the earth."

Of course, our ancestors of the biblical era knew far less about biological complexity than we do today, but one verse evokes the notion that God laid down His blueprint for our bodies on the cellular level. As the Psalmist contemplates our creation in the womb, he reflects on God's awareness of our earliest fleshly incarnation—before our limbs were even formed. From fertilized egg to zygote to fetus, God the designer has seen and directed our development: "Your eyes saw my unformed limbs; they were all recorded in Your book."

What is God's book that records our undeveloped bodily organs and features? Modern biologists have taught us that each cell contains within its core the genetic code for all our physical and mental characteristics: face, shape, hair, limbs, and even some personality traits. Perhaps "God's book" is an unknowing reference to DNA, the secret code for every facet of our psychophysical selves. If so, Psalm 139 reminds us that we can embrace modern medicine's depiction of the fundamental workings of human cells without rejecting God as creator of this unimaginably intricate machinery. Indeed, perceiving God as author of our biological code helps us understand that no matter how far medicine goes in describing the human machine, it is not a machine at all, since God is at work in every cell, molecule, and atom of our being.

Perhaps the most powerful verse for those of us struggling with illness is "I praise You, for I am awesomely, wondrously made; Your work is wonderful; I know it very well." Anyone who has recovered from a serious illness comes to appreciate the wonder of the healing process. How do our tissues knit together so seamlessly? How can the immune system regularly mount battles of staggering breadth and complexity in order to rid the body of foreign invaders, then clean up the remnants of battle so thoroughly that we feel few ill effects? How is it possible for the body to heal after a cardiothoracic surgeon has sawed open the chest and held the heart in his hands?

I know something of the miracle of recovery from open-heart surgery. After my own coronary bypass operation, I was taken aback by the severity of the discomfort. When I came home from the hospital, every fiber of my being seemed suffused with pain. I lay on the couch, unable to climb the stairs to my bedroom. Even shaving was a strenuous affair. My strength for every aspect of living—moving, speaking, relating—was virtually gone. I lost many pounds along with my appetite. At one point, my wife called my cardiologist and told him the extent of my pain, to which he said, "This is an unfortunate but normal part of his recuperation. It's as if he's been hit by a 2-ton truck." The physical pain was bad enough, but the emotional distress was devastating. I was afraid that I would never recover my old self—my mobility, energy, and capacity to work.

Then, slowly, bit by bit, my strength began to revive. The first sign was the return of my appetite. Moving from the living room to the kitchen had been a tough excursion, but soon I began to walk around the house as before. I could never have imagined that I would be grateful just to climb the stairs to my bedroom without crushing pain and exhaustion. As my energy and vitality returned, like currents of water over a dry riverbed, I thought about how awesomely, wondrously, God has made our bodies.

I also thought about the marvel of modern cardiothoracic surgery. My surgeon used chemicals to stop the beating of my heart, then turned its functions over to a machine so he could carefully sew veins removed from my legs onto its surface, bypassing the blockages in my own arteries. But the miracles of medicine would be useless without the miracle of my body's own healing abilities. After the surgeon is finished, the body takes over: Grafts hold, blood courses through new veins, and the sheared skin, muscle, and bone are rewoven. Doctor and patient have joined forces to take full advantage of that which only the patient can do—restore tissues and organs to their normal functions through an exquisite process of self-repair.

The spirit needs repair too. I found myself in dark moments of depression after my surgery—especially when I was so weak, but also later on. The depression began when I was frightened of long-term incapacity, but I didn't understand all its causes or dimensions. I asked my cardiologist if he could arrange for me to see a psychiatrist at the hospital, and he readily complied.

The psychiatrist was immensely reassuring: "This is what most everyone feels after open-heart surgery." I was eminently relieved merely to know that what I was experiencing was normal. We need to understand that our suffering is not a strange aberration. When we know this, we become connected with others in the same boat, which helps us to feel less alone. The psychiatrist's counsel was a simple act of care with great consequence for my well-being.

Modern mind-body research tells us that the brain and the heart, once believed to be as disconnected as the hood and trunk of an automobile, are in fact intimately connected. Nerve branches and chemicals link the two, and some studies suggest that the heart sends messages to the brain as surely as the brain sends messages to the heart. This offers us hints as to why we become depressed when our hearts, the loci of love and compassion, must recover from the insult of being shut down, exposed, and revived after a mini-death.

Still, my cardiologist told me that, once I had recovered, it would be as if my heart were 20 years younger. As I began to feel surges of vitality, I told my wife, Janet, "Be careful, because I am now 20 years younger than you!" I know that my heart has bounced back from the insult of surgery. If the heart can be said to have a mind, my heart is grateful for the veins that now keep it strong and supple.

Having come through this experience of open-heart surgery, I now truly understand the verse "for I am awesomely, wondrously made; Your work is wonderful; I know it very well."

The Psalmist, having contemplated God's omnipresence and His creation of the body, proclaims his awe at the weight and number of God's thoughts: "I count them— they exceed the grains of sand." As human beings, we can hold only a finite number of thoughts at one time; we can concentrate only on a few people or problems. But God can keep all of us in mind, the billions of us on Earth who work and love, exult and suffer, grow sick and get well. How He is present for each one of us is a mystery. But there it is, a timeless truth in the great religious and spiritual traditions.

"I end—but am still with You": This is a verse with many meanings, all of which carry the same conclusion. My skin ends, but that does not keep me separate from God. My life ends, but that does not keep me separate from God. My feelings, thoughts, and physical capacities are finite, but that does not keep me separate from God. God lays His hand on each one of us, throughout sickness, health, life, death, eternity.

PSALM 27

◆ ◆ ◆

TO LET OUR HEARTS
TAKE COURAGE

Look to the Lord;

be strong and
of good courage!

O look to the Lord!

To Let Our Hearts
Take Courage

PSALM 27

The Lord is my light and my help;
  whom should I fear?
The Lord is the stronghold of my life,
  whom should I dread?
When evil men assail me
  to devour my flesh —
  it is they, my foes and my enemies,
  who stumble and fall.
Should an army besiege me,
  my heart would have no fear;
  should war beset me,
  still would I be confident.

One thing I ask of the Lord,
  only that do I seek:
  to live in the house of the Lord
  all the days of my life,

to gaze upon the beauty of the Lord,
to frequent His temple.
He will shelter me in His pavilion
on an evil day,
grant me the protection of His tent,
raise me high upon a rock.
Now is my head high
over my enemies roundabout;
I sacrifice in His tent with shouts of joy,
singing and chanting a hymn to the Lord.

Hear, O Lord, when I cry aloud;
have mercy on me, answer me.
In Your behalf my heart says:
"Seek My face!"
O Lord, I seek Your face.
Do not hide Your face from me;
do not thrust aside Your servant
in anger;
You have ever been my help.
Do not forsake me, do not abandon me,
O God, my deliverer.
Though my father and mother abandon me,
the Lord will take me in.
Show me Your way, O Lord,
and lead me on a level path
because of my watchful foes.
Do not subject me to the will of my foes,
for false witnesses and unjust accusers
have appeared against me.

Had I not the assurance
  that I would enjoy the goodness of the Lord
  in the land of the living . . .

Look to the Lord;
  be strong and of good courage!
O look to the Lord!

Those of us overtaken by the darkness of illness, depression, or grief may feel like prisoners of war. When we are in that much pain and fear, we feel isolated even if we are not alone. We feel attacked from without, even if we are being attacked only from within. We may feel unjustly treated, even if we are victims of bad fortune more than bad treatment by others. Having been struck with disease, remanded to our beds, and subjected to arduous treatments, we are thrust into a seemingly helpless position, one against which we rail in the hope of an ultimate escape.

Psalm 27 offers God as a beacon of hope and confidence when we feel surrounded, imprisoned, or overtaken. No matter what our circumstances, Psalm 27 reminds us that we can look to the Lord for light and courage. As I wrote in the introduction, when Natan Sharansky spent 9 years as a political prisoner in a Russian jail cell, long before the breakup of the Soviet Union, he held tight to his Book of

Psalms as a spiritual source of strength. Fearful that his captors would take away his book, Sharansky memorized Psalm 27, with its opening verse, "The Lord is my light and my help; whom should I fear?"

For some, the experience of life-threatening illness is akin to being a prisoner of war. For others, it's more like being a refugee on the run. Psalm 27 is apparently derived from the story of David and his flight from Saul. After the young lad killed mighty Goliath with his slingshot, he was even more intensely favored by Saul, the first king of Israel. David would play his harp for the king, who was subject to deep moods of melancholy. (Today, we would say that David applied music therapy to Saul's clinical depression.) David became a great warrior, slaying more Philistines in battle than Saul did, so it was David who received the most ardent songs of salutation from the legions of women awaiting their return from battle. Motivated by jealousy, Saul turned on David and began his epic pursuit of the boy who would be king. David was perpetually in flight from his pursuer, who had become maniacally obsessed with David's demise.

According to many scholars, Psalm 27 is all about David's torment at Saul's persecution and about his turning to God for protection and sustenance. "When evil men assail me to devour my flesh—it is they, my foes and my enemies, who stumble and fall. . . . He will shelter me in His pavilion on an evil day." The "pavilion" is described by 19th-century biblical scholar Samson Raphael Hirsch: "The Tabernacle, though it be a simple hut, is considered safe shelter for me for it encompasses His presence even as it surrounds my own person."

The Psalmist asks for the Lord's shelter "all the days of my life," echoing a similar verse in the more famous Psalm 23. No matter what calamities befall us, we can seek and receive God's safekeeping forever. God lifts us up above our enemies, where we can "sacrifice in His tent with shouts of joy, singing and chanting a hymn to the Lord." Many of the Psalms were sung in the temple as hosannas, such as Psalm 150: "Praise Him with timbrel and dance; praise him with lute and pipe. Praise Him with resounding cymbals. . . . Let all that breathes praise the Lord." The ancients used the Psalms as lyrics for a magnificent blend of instruments and human voices that built toward a great musical crescendo, like the chorus of Beethoven's Ninth Symphony.

Psalm 27 moves from celebration back to poignant seeking, as in a musical piece that returns to its plaintive theme. "Hear, O Lord, when I cry aloud; have mercy on me, answer me." In his anguish, the Psalmist is neither reticent nor silent; he wants God's attention. Then comes one of the most interesting turns of phrase in the Book of Psalms: "In Your behalf my heart says: 'Seek My face!'" It's a fascinating linguistic twist: The heart is speaking on behalf of God, telling the Psalmist to seek God's face. It implies that we hear God's voice if we listen intently to our own hearts. When ill, frightened, or grief-stricken, we can look within for guidance from the Almighty. And in Psalm 27, what do our hearts, and God, tell us? Do not be meek, timid, or subservient. Find God, however you must. Request God's protective presence; be certain that He does not forsake or abandon you.

When we are sick, some of us have all the loving support we need. Others wish for more support. But whether or not we have many caring friends and family members, we are bound to feel alone with our suffering at least on occasion. We may even feel let down by some friends and family members who have not "shown up" as we've wished them to. While support systems are rarely perfect and sometimes sadly inadequate, God is steadfast. "Though my father and mother abandon me, the Lord will take me in." Father and mother could stand for any member of a support network who is absent or inconstant in his or her support.

Isolation, abandonment, and even hostile attacks, the banes of prisoners and refugees, can also be the misfortune of those of us who are sick. But the attacks we face are rarely from others, unless we are subjected to insults or neglect based on the stigma associated with a particular disease. As in Psalm 139, the foes that we usually recognize are internal ones, the agents of disease: bacteria, viruses, cancer cells. "Do not subject me to the will of my foes." When stricken, we often feel that we've been unjustly attacked, whether by disease agents, fate, or some woeful combination of both. But the beauty of Psalm 27 is that it transforms victimhood into agency: We are never powerless against unjust attacks, since we can turn to God.

It may be too much to expect ourselves to manage the stress and pain of severe illness without a spiritual bulwark. "Had I not the assurance that I would enjoy the goodness of the Lord in the land of the living . . .": The verse is left unfinished, which is extremely rare in biblical writings. The thought of not being able to trust in God's goodness, especially when besieged and threatened, is too terrible to even contemplate. There are no words for the Psalmist's imagined despair. (In this instance, *no words* create a more powerful effect than any words could.) Just as a person recovering from illness might say, "I don't know how I would have made it without my wife," the Psalmist is saying, "I don't know how I would have made it without God."

The final verse is among the most empowering in the Book of Psalms. The protagonist—David, or any other person fending off a mortal threat—finds safety and redemption in faith. "Look to the Lord; be strong and of good courage! O look to the Lord!" These words ring with an indomitable optimism. The root of the Hebrew word for *look* is actually closer to *hope*. It's the core message of Psalm 27: Hope in the Lord. What every sick person and family member yearns for is hope: hope for recovery, hope for the courage to endure, hope that God will be present in our lives no matter what happens.

During the Korean War, I was a chaplain in the army. I was the first full-time Jewish chaplain stationed at Fort Belvoir in Virginia. Thousands of young kids came through Fort Belvoir, some of whom would receive the dreaded news that they were headed for the service in Korea. There were lists on the wall in each barracks with either *Eucom* for European command or *Fecom* for Far East command, and the 18-year-old soldiers would regularly check the lists with trepidation in their hearts. They tried not to show it, but many of these kids were scared to death. They felt that they were heading into the maw of destruction.

For me, it was an age-old problem, one that confronts any member of the clergy. I could say, "Get a Bible and read it," but what good would that do? A man or woman full of fear cannot possibly know where to find solace in the Five Books of Moses, or any other great book of worship, for that matter. So I simply told the frightened young men to read Psalm 27. The words "Look to the Lord; be strong and of good courage!" must have resonated for them. A number of boys wrote out the Psalm on a piece of paper, folded it up, and tucked it into their shirt pockets. Some took it with them to the Korean front.

Anyone stuck in a place of uncertainty and fear may find comfort and courage in Psalm 27. I think about cancer patients, who must wait for news of diagnostic tests; have their arms stuck with needles for administration of toxic chemotherapy drugs; and endure the nausea, fatigue, and other distressing side effects of treatment. I think of patients with any life-threatening or debilitating disease—AIDS, heart disease, diabetes, or neuromuscular disease, to name a few. When we battle any of these conditions and the side effects of therapy, we gain needed strength from loved ones and from God, our light and our help, the stronghold of our lives.

PSALM 31

♦ ♦ ♦

TO EASE SHAME AND SORROW

Into Your hand I entrust my spirit;

You redeem me,

O Lord, faithful God.

To Ease Shame and Sorrow

Psalm 31

◆　◆　◆

I seek refuge in You, O Lord;
*   may I never be disappointed;*
*   as You are righteous, rescue me.*
Incline Your ear to me;
*   be quick to save me;*
*   be a rock, a stronghold for me,*
*   a citadel, for my deliverance.*
For You are my rock and my fortress;
*   You lead me and guide me as befits Your name.*
You free me from the net laid for me,
*   for You are my stronghold.*
Into Your hand I entrust my spirit;
*   You redeem me, O Lord, faithful God. . . .*
Let me exult and rejoice in Your faithfulness
*   when You notice my affliction,*
*   are mindful of my deep distress,*
*   and do not hand me over to my enemy,*
*   but grant me relief.*

Have mercy on me, O Lord,
  for I am in distress;
  my eyes are wasted by vexation,
  my substance and body too.
My life is spent in sorrow,
  my years in groaning;
  my strength fails because of my iniquity,
  my limbs waste away.
Because of all my foes
  I am the particular butt of my neighbors,
  a horror to my friends;
  those who see me on the street avoid me.
I am put out of mind like the dead;
  I am like an object given up for lost. . . .

But I trust in You, O Lord;
  I say, "You are my God!". . .
Show favor to Your servant;
  as You are faithful, deliver me.
O Lord, let me not be disappointed when I call
    You;
  let the wicked be disappointed;
  let them be silenced in Sheol [the nether-
    world];
  let lying lips be stilled
  that speak haughtily against the righteous
  with arrogance and contempt. . . .
Blessed is the Lord,
  for He has been wondrously faithful to me,
  a veritable bastion.

Alarmed, I had thought,
  "I am thrust out of Your sight";
    yet You listened to my plea for mercy
    when I cried out to You.
So love the Lord, all you faithful;
  the Lord guards the loyal,
  and more than requites
  him who acts arrogantly.
Be strong and of good courage,
  all you who wait for the Lord.

The compassionate God, protector of the afflicted, the abandoned, and the stigmatized, emerges in Psalm 31. Here, the Lord is a rock and a fortress, the ultimate port of safe harbor. When doctors, nurses, parents, children, brothers, sisters, or friends fail us, as they sometimes will, the Lord is still with us. But most important, when lost in private terrors, whether from pain or the abject fear of our own mortality, we can turn our anguish over to Him. Among the most stirring verses in the entire Psalter is "Into Your hand I entrust my spirit; You redeem me, O Lord, faithful God."

Although it is a "Psalm of David" with historical overtones, Psalm 31 is described by the authors of the translation in the *Soncino Books of the Bible* as "written for the benefit of anyone who might find it necessary to reaffirm his belief that God can extricate him from any predicament." The Psalm is certainly laden with predicaments; it depicts a world in which traps are set, nets are laid, and nefarious forces encircle the Psalmist. Yet the Psalmist turns to God in a voice of confident yearning, certain that he will find deliverance.

While ill will abounds, the precise cause of the Psalmist's pleas for rescue and redemption are not clear. By the 10th verse, however, one reason is made apparent: He suffers from a serious illness that leaves his eyes and body "wasted by vexation," his limbs withered, his spirits depleted. Physical suffering is accompanied by the sting of social rejection: "I am the particular butt of my neighbors, a horror to my friends; those who see me on the street avoid me."

Here, the pain of stigma is captured in verses as succinct and powerful as any in the vast literature of illness. In modern times, these words summon the specter of cancer and AIDS, diseases that have long been saddled with negative cultural baggage. Until fairly recently, the word *cancer* was hardly utterable. Cancer was a source of shame for the patient and his or her family because it was wrongly believed to be either infectious or a sign of spiritual impoverishment. Another fallacious belief, that cancer was a

certain death sentence, also led to stigmatization as society's denial of death was projected onto sick patients
through a lens of fear and misunderstanding. (Today, more
than half of all cancer patients will be cured, and certain
types of cancer are completely curable.) AIDS, known
from the start of the epidemic to be infectious, was
thought to be spread through incidental contact, and suf-
ferers were treated as pariahs. We now know that AIDS
cannot be transmitted through casual contact, but stigma
continues in the form of fear and loathing of people who
belong to "behavioral risk groups."

The persistence of stigma, albeit in less malign forms,
with both of these diseases mirrors past and present social
responses to many other infectious diseases, disabilities,
and deformities. "In certain societies, so powerful is the
stigma brought to the patient by the culturally marked illness label that it affects all his relationships and may lead
to ostracism," says Harvard psychiatrist Arthur Kleinman,
M.D., in his book *The Illness Narratives*. If we look deeper
into society's attitudes, we find individuals seeking to distance themselves not from a transmissible disease but from
people—sometimes loved ones—whose illnesses mirror
their vulnerability and whose presence elicits difficult
emotions they wish to banish from consciousness.

It is often hard to know what to say to those we love who are sick. Often, we are overwhelmed by our own feelings. I recall a man in my former congregation, a physician named Howard, whose best friend, Jeff, had been diagnosed with advanced cancer. Jeff's wife, Ellen, was distraught when she reported to me that Howard had not once come to visit Jeff. Ellen could not understand how Howard's closest friend, a physician no less, could be so shamelessly neglectful. Howard must have known how much pain this was causing Jeff. I met with Howard and shared with him what Ellen had told me. He was deeply embarrassed, confessing, "Rabbi, the reason I haven't visited Jeff is simple. I'm afraid that I'll collapse. I can manage with my patients, but with a friend as close as Jeff, I'm afraid that I'll break down and won't be any help to him."

I encouraged Howard to visit Jeff despite his fears, but he was unable to do so. Weeks later, I ran into Howard in an elevator while on my way to visit Jeff. He asked if we could speak, and when he took me aside, he confided that he continued to agonize over visiting Jeff. I asked why it would be so terrible for him to break down. "He'll read my tears as a sign that I believe there's no hope for him, and I don't want to inflict that pain."

"On the contrary," I said, "if you do cry, Jeff will see this as an act of love. I think your visit will help him and Ellen, no matter what."

After a moment's contemplation, Howard replied, "I'll visit him right now, but I need you to be there. I can't do it alone."

When we entered Jeff's hospital room, Ellen was there, and as soon as she saw Howard, she stormed out. But Jeff didn't let anger sabotage this opportunity. The two men shed unabashed tears and hugged, and I left soon so that they could have privacy. Howard began visiting Jeff every day, sometimes twice a day. The pain of abandonment and fear had been healed, and although Jeff would live for only 2 more weeks, the two men found peace in their renewed friendship. At Jeff's funeral, Howard approached Ellen to explain and apologize for his neglect. She had been too full of rage to accept his change of heart before, but she now offered him her forgiveness, and they embraced. During shivah, the mourning period, Howard called to thank me. "Thank you for encouraging me. If I hadn't gone to see Jeff, I never would have let myself off the hook."

Howard had thought that he was protecting his friend by not visiting him, but I sensed that he was protecting himself from his own grief and anxiety. Jeff grasped this intuitively, which enabled him to forgive his longtime friend for an otherwise inexplicable lapse. Transcending barriers of defensiveness, they healed the breach in their relationship, which then became a source of sustenance for Jeff in his final days and allowed Howard to forgive himself for his earlier weakness.

Patients and members of patients' support systems must often work hard to overcome their anxieties so that they can come together when illness strikes. I often find that loved ones develop a stiff psychological armor based on their own fears. They don't always overcome their defenses, and when they don't, they leave the ill person feeling abandoned or ostracized. Through open communication and a willingness to look deeper into others' motives, patients and loved ones may heal the separateness that causes so much suffering. But when some members of the support system can't move beyond their fears, the patient must look to others and to an abiding faith within.

Patients may also suffer when friends or family adopt the wrongheaded societal attitude that disease is caused by a character deficit, a failing of the will or spirit. Susan Sontag helps to dispel these harmful myths in her book *Illness as Metaphor*. Sontag attacks the use of cancer and other diseases as metaphors for personality flaws, spiritual inadequacy, or worse. "The modern disease metaphors are all cheap shots," she writes. "The people who have the real disease are hardly helped by hearing their disease's name constantly being dropped as the epitome of evil."

These attitudes are changing, and someday, education will eradicate them from our minds and hearts. In our desire to label a disease "the enemy," we must be careful not to confuse the sickness with the subject. Like the longed-for cancer drug that destroys malignant cells without harming normal ones, we can wage a psychological fight against disease without also targeting the stricken. Patients and loved ones must resist the idea that people wish disease upon themselves or that their ailments result from character deficiencies. Yes, certain diseases are caused, caught, or worsened by certain behaviors (such as sexual contact, drug use, alcohol, and smoking), by stress, or even by emotional factors. But it does not follow that illness is therefore a punishment or that people are wholly responsible for their diseases. Behavior is only one factor in illness; genes and environmental exposure play critical roles, too. We must also recognize that improper education, bad childhood experiences, and emotional vulnerabilities are underlying causes of addictions and behaviors that *can* contribute to illness. Should sick people be blamed for their illnesses, or blame themselves, simply because they are human?

Can't we take responsibility for our health without denigrating ourselves for every behavioral blemish?

We can use prayer, and the Psalms in particular, for liberation from the impulse to heap scorn on ourselves and our loved ones. "On the globe of the microcosm the flow of prayer is like the Gulf Stream, imparting warmth to all that is cold, melting all that is hard in our life," writes Abraham Joshua Heschel in *I Asked for Wonder*. "For even loyalties may freeze to indifference if detached from the stream which carries the strength to be loyal. How often does justice lapse into cruelty, and righteousness into hypocrisy. Prayer revives and keeps alive the rare greatness of some past experience in which things glowed with meaning and blessing."

For Heschel, prayer is the stream that carries the strength to be loyal, whether to ourselves, in the form of self-love and self-forgiveness, or to others, in the form of nonjudgmental acceptance of their ailments and vulnerabilities. The verses of Psalm 31 tap into that stream, and they melt all that is hard in our lives.

For the afflicted person, disease should be no source of shame, but it can be a spur to behavioral change, a call to personal transformation, and an opportunity to find meaning. The emotional and physical anguish that attends disease also can lead us to seek union with the Almighty.

In Psalm 31, the Psalmist turns to God with his shame and suffering. The verse "I seek refuge in You, O Lord; may I never be disappointed" is translated differently in the Soncino version: "In Thee, O Lord, have I taken refuge; *let me never be ashamed*" (italics added). Yes, God instills us with a moral conscience, but He also protects us from disgrace over our frailties. "Let me exult and rejoice in Your faithfulness when You notice my affliction, are mindful of my deep distress, and do not hand me over to my enemy, but grant me relief." God notices our afflictions and is mindful of our deep distress. We are not isolated in our anguish, even if others remain separate out of fear. We trust in His loving-kindness, as He can grant us relief—if not from our physical troubles then from our sense of separateness from the Divine.

In the Psalm's key transition, we discover that turning to God can purge us of self-loathing over disease. "I am put out of mind like the dead; I am like an object given up for lost. . . . But I trust in You, O Lord; I say, 'You are my God!'" Even when others keep distant and the world has cast a reproachful eye, we are not abandoned. We may be judged mercilessly by fragile brothers and sisters, but not by the Almighty. "Alarmed, I had thought, 'I am thrust out of Your sight'; yet You listened to my plea for mercy when I cried out to You."

This exquisite Psalm gives voice to the yearning of the sick for Divine relief from the sting of shame and the sorrow of loneliness. But it offers more: a final, ringing verse of inspiration so pristine that it deserves to be a mantra for those who struggle with illness or whose loved ones are struggling: "Be strong and of good courage, all you who wait for the Lord."

PSALM 34

◆ ◆ ◆

TO MEND OUR
BROKEN HEARTS

The Lord is close to the brokenhearted;

those crushed in spirit

He delivers.

To Mend Our
Broken Hearts

Psalm 34

I bless the Lord at all times;
   praise of Him is ever in my mouth.
I glory in the Lord;
   let the lowly hear it and rejoice.
Exalt the Lord with me;
   let us extol His name together.
I turned to the Lord, and He answered me;
   He saved me from all my terrors.
Men look to Him and are radiant;
   let their faces not be downcast.
Here was a lowly man who called,
   and the Lord listened,
   and delivered him from all his troubles. . . .
Taste and see how good the Lord is;
   happy the man who takes refuge in Him! . . .
Who is the man who is eager for life,
   who desires years of good fortune?

Guard your tongue from evil,
  your lips from deceitful speech.
Shun evil and do good,
  seek amity and pursue it.
The eyes of the Lord are on the righteous,
  His ears attentive to their cry. . . .
They cry out, and the Lord hears,
  and saves them from all their troubles.
The Lord is close to the brokenhearted;
  those crushed in spirit He delivers.
Though the misfortunes of the righteous be
    many,
  the Lord will save him from them all, . . .

The voice in Psalm 34 rings with resounding force and clarity, in a poem of celebration more than petition. The Psalmist does not beseech God as much as he praises the Almighty for His help and, ultimately, for the salvation that we will receive. This God is compassionate, safeguarding the "lowly," the brokenhearted. One way to read the message of this Psalm is that God does not act to protect the "lowly" and "righteous" from all suffering, but, rather, He delivers us from the spiritual wasteland of loneliness, detachment, and disillusionment in the midst of suffering.

We "bless," "exalt," and "glory in" the Lord not just during the Sabbath, on Sundays, or during holidays but "at all times." A true spiritual enlightenment involves gratitude for the presence of the Absolute in every moment of our lives. Turning to the Lord saves the Psalmist from his terrors but not, as we shall later see, from actual misfortune. While the Psalms may be open to countless interpretations, Psalm 34 intimates that we turn to the Lord not to stave off bad events but to rescue us from an emotional and spiritual desert in the face of bad events. The Lord listened to the "lowly man"—defined by one biblical scholar as the "afflicted man." (We might assume any affliction, including poverty, alienation, and disease.) A hint that God does not vanquish all poverty and illness, but rather transforms our experience of suffering, is resonant in this verse: "Men look to Him and are radiant; let their faces not be downcast."

Men and women don't become radiant because their lives are made perfect by God; they become radiant through the experience of God. Modern-day psychologists point out that no one escapes stress and trauma. Our health and well-being turns on the question, how do we *respond* to stress and trauma? Psalm 34 suggests that without God, we may lapse into despair. With God, we still endure grief and loss, but we do not succumb to hopelessness.

But how do we look to God? Simply by believing? By

reading about theology and religion? By going to a church, mosque, or synagogue? The answer may include all of the above, but it must be more. In one verse, we glimpse an answer: "Taste and see how good the Lord is; happy the man who takes refuge in Him!" The word *taste* here is key. The Psalmist does not ask us to ponder God, talk to God, or connect with God. He asks us to *experience* the Almighty. We can "taste" the Lord's goodness through meditation, prayer, or other practices that put us directly in touch with Him.

What does it mean to move beyond *knowledge about* God to *experience of* God? In his book *Man Is Not Alone*, Abraham Joshua Heschel refers to the pious man who tastes rather than thinks about God:

> To the pious man God is as real as life, and as nobody would be satisfied with mere knowing or reading about life, so he is not content to suppose or prove logically that there is a God; he wants to feel and to give himself to Him; not only to obey but to approach Him. His desire is to taste the whole wheat of spirit before it is ground by the millstone of reason. He would rather be overwhelmed by the symbols of the inconceivable than wield the definitions of the superficial.

> Stirred by a yearning after the unattainable, a pious man

is not content with being confined to what he is. His desire is not only to know more than ordinary reason has to offer, but to be more than what he is; to transform the soul into a vessel for the transcendent, to grasp with the senses what is hidden from the mind, to express in symbols what the tongue cannot speak and what reason cannot conceive, to experience as a reality what vaguely dawns in intuition.

So direct experience of God is not gained through the intellect but through a direct grasp of what Heschel and others call the ineffable. No words can really capture it. The oratory of theologians who try to prove God's existence is usually dry as dust. From a Jewish perspective, Heschel has found a poetic language that comes closest to transcendent truths about the Absolute. A similar regard for the ineffable can be found in other religious traditions.

In his book *One Taste*, philosopher Ken Wilber refers to the experience of oneness at the heart of all great religious and spiritual traditions. Here he discusses that state achieved after deep meditation:

You still have complete access to the waking-state ego, but you are no longer only that. Rather, the very deepest part of you is one with the entire Kosmos in all its radiant glory. You simply are everything that is arising moment to moment. You do not see the sky, you are the sky. You do not touch the earth, you are the earth. You do not hear the rain, you are the rain. You and the universe are what the mystics call "One Taste." This is not poetry. This is a direct realization, as direct as a glass of cold water in the face. . . .

As researchers from Aldous Huxley to Huston Smith have reminded us, One Taste or cosmic consciousness—the sense of oneness with the ground of all creation—is the deepest core of the nearly universal consensus of the world's great wisdom traditions. One Taste is not a hallucination, fantasy, or product of a disturbed psyche, but the direct realization and testament of countless yogis, saints, and sages the world over. It is very simple, very obvious, very clear—concrete, palpable, unmistakable.

Wilber's description of this concrete and palpable sense of oneness echoes the Psalmist's use of the word *taste*. Touch, feel, taste: Our oneness with God ought to suffuse every aspect of our being, not just our cerebral cortex.

The Psalm's next section starts with an interesting question: "Who is the man who is eager for life, who desires years of good fortune?" In a previous translation by the

Jewish Publication Society, the question reads: "Who is the man that desireth life, and *loveth days*, that he may see good therein?" Those of us who are sick recognize the need to appreciate every moment and day of our lives, since we have come to realize their preciousness. But what enables us to "love days"?

The Psalm offers one suggestion: "Guard your tongue from evil, your lips from deceitful speech." Biblical writings often refer to the power of words either to heal or to harm. For instance, we can readily understand the awesome power that doctors hold with their words: An optimistic remark buoys our spirits, while a negative comment can send us reeling into despair for days or even months.

One of my doctors is Bernard Lown, M.D., a distinguished cardiologist who wrote about the power of words in his book, *The Lost Art of Healing*. Dr. Lown worries about "words that maim," and he offers examples used by other doctors as reported by his patients: "You are living on borrowed time." "You have a time bomb in your chest." "You can have a heart attack any minute." A cardiology consultant pointed to an obstructed artery on a coronary angiogram and informed a patient's wife, "This narrow blood vessel is a widow maker."

But it is not just the physician's words that are consequential when it comes to healing. The patient's own words matter too. How, you might ask, could your own utterances influence your recovery from disease? According to a substantial body of research, people who habitually use hostile words and gestures, who explode with anger when stressed, may be more prone to heart disease and even severe heart attacks.

Redford Williams, M.D., of Duke University in Durham, North Carolina, is an acknowledged leader of research on hostility and heart disease. "Extensive research has shown that hostility, lack of social support, and high job stress increase the likelihood of developing cardiovascular disease and dying from it prematurely," says Dr. Williams. Of course, not all people with heart disease have troubles with anger, but many do, and their psychological tendencies play a part in their illnesses.

How strong is the link? One of Dr. Williams's colleagues at Duke, Dr. John Barefoot, of the department of psychology and behavioral science, evaluated data on doctors and lawyers who had been tracked for 25 years. Doctors who scored high on a test for hostility were four to five times more likely to develop heart disease than those who were not hostile. The hostility test measured a cynical mistrust of people, the frequent experience of anger, and the overt expression of aggressive behavior in deeds and words. In another study, researchers found a slightly increased risk of cancer among individuals with a greater tendency for hostility.

"There is growing evidence that learning to become less hostile and angry, and developing stronger networks of social support, can improve the prognosis for many people with coronary disease," writes Dr. Williams. This approach may also help prevent people from developing heart disease in the first place. In his book *Anger Kills*, Dr. Williams and his wife, Virginia, offer 17 strategies people can use to become less hostile. Among them: "Stop Hostile Thoughts, Feelings, and Urges," "Distract Yourself," "Practice Trusting Others," "Take On Community Service," "Be Tolerant," "Forgive," and "Become More Religious."

In other words, "Guard your tongue from evil, your lips from deceitful speech. Shun evil and do good, seek amity and pursue it." Such a commitment may be good not only for your soul—enabling you to "love days"—but also for your health.

The final verses of Psalm 34 remind us in powerful prose that God attends to the cries of those in pain. Among the noblest and most stirring sentiments in the entire Book of Psalms is "The Lord is close to the brokenhearted; those crushed in spirit He delivers."

Whether we suffer or a loved one suffers from heart disease, cancer, or any other serious illness, the experience may leave us brokenhearted. Bad news beckons, and our hopes for future health and happiness can be shattered. At precisely these moments, we need the wisdom and truth contained in Psalm 34—that God is close to the brokenhearted, that He delivers us when our spirits are crushed. There is a beautiful midrash, or narrative elaboration, by Rabbi Alexandri, a 3rd-century sage, that expands on this idea: "When man uses a broken vessel, he is ashamed of it, but not so God. All the instruments of His service are broken vessels, as it is written: 'The Lord is close to them that have a broken heart.'"

The same notion is apparent in a midrash about Moses' destruction of the tablets containing the Ten Commandments. When Moses descended from Mount Sinai with the tablets, he witnessed the Israelites worshipping the golden calf. He promptly smashed the tablets in a fit of rage. (The ancients knew nothing of anger management.) Moses then scaled Mount Sinai again to retrieve a new set of tablets to bring to his people. According to the midrash, God considered the broken tablets just as holy as the unbroken ones, which is why Moses placed the shards in the same ark with the restored tablets. Interpreters made much of this metaphor: God cares as much for the broken as for the whole.

How many of us escape life intact? Life breaks all of us in some way or another. Even our healers are wounded. (Carl Jung spoke of "wounded healers": Doctors, psychiatrists, and clergypeople are often as brokenhearted as those they counsel.) But how do we live with and transcend our heartbreak? It's up to us. We can let heartbreak destroy our spirits and drive us deeper into alienation and illness. (In Saul Bellow's novel *More Die of Heartbreak*, a botanist is asked by a reporter about radioactive pollution. "It's terribly serious, of course," replies the botanist. "But I think more people die of heartbreak. . . . ") Or heartbreak can make us wiser, more empathic human beings, bringing us closer to the compassionate God whose praises are sung in this Psalm.

A strange, iconoclastic figure in Jewish history, the Rabbi of Kotzk, once made the paradoxical comment, "Nothing is as whole as a broken heart." Perhaps he meant that heartbreak can make us more caring, smarter, holier—not in a self-pitying or self-satisfied way, but through the humble recognition of our common humanity, the basis for a richly creative and authentic life. In his stunning memoir of his early life in Ireland, *Angela's Ashes*, Frank

McCourt wrote, "When I look back on my childhood I wonder how I managed to survive at all. It was, of course, a miserable childhood: the happy childhood is hardly worth your while."

McCourt is himself a good example of someone who turned the dross of a miserable childhood into the gold of a creative adulthood—not only because his book was a bestseller that made him wealthy but also because his book was a vibrant work of art that will endure for ages. How many great figures in politics, art, and science have transmogrified their suffering into lives of meaning and contribution? Some have used physical disease or disability not as a crutch but as a stimulus for extraordinary transformation. Ludwig van Beethoven, Franklin Delano Roosevelt, Stephen Hawking, and Christopher Reeve come to mind.

I recently saw a documentary on the life of Senator Max Cleland of Georgia, *Strong at the Broken Places*. Cleland was a 26-year-old Army captain in Vietnam when his limbs were shattered by a grenade. He managed to rebuild his life, becoming director of the Veterans Administration before winning his Senate seat.

"Hemingway was right," said Senator Cleland in the film. "Life breaks us all. But many are strong at the broken places, and that's one of the things I've learned. By the grace of God and the help of friends, it is possible to become strong even at the broken places."

We can respond to any hardship this way, though the path to metamorphosis may be as hard as nails. Perhaps we should view God not as a balm for the brokenhearted but as a beacon lighting the way toward that hard-won transformation. *Shadowlands*, a play about the Christian theorist and poet C. S. Lewis, helps us understand how difficult this can be. According to the playwright, William Nicholson, Lewis has an intellectual grasp of the transformative potential of suffering: "We're like blocks of stone," says the Lewis character, "out of which the sculptor carves the forms of men. The blows of his chisel, which hurt us so much, are what make us perfect. The suffering in the world is not the failure of God's love for us; it is that love in action."

But Lewis himself sidestepped the blows of real life by hiding in the cocoon of ivory-tower academia. When he fell in love with an American poet and she succumbed to cancer, Lewis finally had to face up to his theories. "He had been advocating pain as something which actually makes you a better person," said the actor Nigel Hawthorne, who played Lewis on Broadway. "And it is turned right back in his face." Yet Lewis was ultimately redeemed as he learned to live an authentic life. He moved through rapturous joy and searing loss, finally coming to grasp what it means to love someone, to taste rather than talk about the Divine.

The verse "Though the misfortunes of the righteous be many, the Lord will save him from them all" presents another paradox. If righteous people are hit with many misfortunes, how is it that the Lord saves them "from them all?" We can only conclude that the Lord does not *prevent* the righteous from experiencing painful events. That's not how the world works. Rather, He saves them from the horrific consequences of those events—spiritual isolation, meaninglessness, bitterness, or terror that never stops. That is the Psalmist's salvation, and that is our salvation. It's also the message of Rabbi Harold Kushner in his famous book *When Bad Things Happen to Good People*. God does not rig the cosmos to reward the righteous, but He offers us all the gift of redemption. That gift is ours when we "taste and see how good the Lord is"—especially when our hearts are broken.

PSALM 90

◆ ◆ ◆

TO TREASURE EACH DAY

Teach us to count our days rightly,

that we may obtain

a wise heart.

TO TREASURE EACH DAY

PSALM 90

◆ ◆ ◆

A prayer of Moses, the man of God.

O Lord, You have been our refuge in every
generation.
Before the mountains came into being,
before You brought forth the earth and the
world,
from eternity to eternity You are God.

You return man to dust;
You decreed, "Return you mortals!"
For in Your sight a thousand years
are like yesterday that has past,
like a watch of the night.
You engulf men in sleep;
at daybreak they are like grass that renews
itself;
at daybreak it flourishes anew;
by dusk it withers and dries up. . . .
we spend our years like a sigh.

The span of our life is seventy years,
  or, given the strength, eighty years;
    but the best of them are trouble and sorrow.
They pass by speedily, and we fly away. . . .
Teach us to count our days rightly,
  that we may obtain a wise heart.

Turn, O Lord!
How long?
Show mercy to Your servants.
Satisfy us at daybreak with Your steadfast love
  that we may sing for joy all our days. . . .
Let Your deeds be seen by Your servants,
  Your glory by their children. . . .

Here is a touchstone for everyone who struggles with life-threatening illness, as either the patient, a family member, or the healer. Psalm 90 emphasizes that time is short, that none of us is immune to stress and sorrow, yet we can "count our days rightly" so that "we may obtain a wise heart." The message that we ought to make the most of our precious days may be a cliché, but for those who are faced with the possibility of a foreshortened life span, it is more than an offhand maxim. It's a truth to be wrestled with.

In the translation of the Book of Psalms found in the *Soncino Books of the Bible*, the commentator writes, "In sub-

lime language this Psalm dwells upon the transitory character of man's existence, but in no pessimistic mood. If life
is brief, its moments are precious and must not be wasted
in vain pursuits. The swift passing of his stay upon earth
would render it meaningless and purposeless, were it not
that God is everlasting and under Him is man's abiding
dwelling-place." The very finitude of life impels us to find
our place in the universe and our relation to God. With
youth comes the illusion of ceaseless health and endless
life. Eventually, when confronted with illness or grief, we
relinquish our denial of death. This affords us an opportunity to deepen our commitment to a life of spiritual realization.

Psalm 90 is a "prayer of Moses," and it alludes to his
struggles. The insecure shepherd with a speech defect was
called upon by God to free his people from Egypt. Facing
the most formidable obstacles one could imagine, he con-
vinces the Israelites that he is God's messenger and leads
the struggle against Pharaoh to liberate them. Although he
succeeds in freeing his people from enslavement, he is
thwarted in his desire to personally lead them to Canaan,
the Promised Land. Scholars argue about the reason that
God kept Moses from the Promised Land, but there is no
doubt that the great liberator, who lived to the ripe age of

120, never realized his fervent dream. Psalm 90 seems like Moses' attempt to put his frustration into spiritual perspective, to appreciate the gifts that God has bestowed. "We spend our years like a sigh," so we should use our time well "that we may sing for joy all our days."

None of us finishes all of our tasks or realizes all of our dreams. But we don't have to allow the unfinished business of our lives to haunt our every waking hour. Perhaps Moses' message is that we can find the wholeness in each moment with a vital mind and an open heart.

In the 20th century, we've heard echoes of Moses in the words of Martin Luther King Jr., particularly in his last speech at a church in Memphis, Tennessee, on the eve of his assassination in 1968. King was in Memphis leading a poor people's march, and he finished his speech with these prophetic, unscripted words:

> We've got some difficult days ahead. But it doesn't matter with me now. Because I've been to the mountaintop. And I don't mind. Like anybody, I would like to live a long life. Longevity has its place. But I'm not concerned about that now. I just want to do God's will. And He's allowed me to go up to the mountain. And I've looked over. And I've seen the Promised Land. I may not get there with you. But I want

you to know tonight, that we, as a people, will get to the Promised Land. And I'm happy, tonight. I'm not worried about anything. I'm not fearing any man. Mine eyes have seen the glory of the coming of the Lord.

King had been to the mountaintop as Moses had been to the mountaintop, having glimpsed the Promised Land from Mount Pisgah before he died. Neither man actually made it to the Promised Land: The people found their own way, though the same struggles have been recapitulated throughout history. Still, both Moses and Martin Luther King Jr. set in motion the liberation of persecuted peoples, having lived lives of commitment to a God of compassion. One achieved longevity while the other did not, but both counted their days rightly and acquired hearts of wisdom.

We shouldn't set our expectations too high—who among us can liberate the multitudes?—but we can define for ourselves a life of meaning and purpose. It may be as simple as being a good mother or father, daughter or son, wife or husband, sister or brother. Or as seemingly mundane as treating the sick or poor people we encounter on the street with kindness and respect. Or as ordinary as working hard at a job that contributes services, products, or artwork to our fellow men and women.

What has this to do with healing and coping? Everything. Many psychotherapists who treat patients with life-threatening illness believe that living a life of purpose and engagement is essential to the healing process. It's no certainty of cure, but it is central to emotional and spiritual healing, which is sometimes associated with physical recovery. The leading proponent of "meaning therapy" for cancer patients is Lawrence LeShan, Ph.D., whose 40 years of experience have led him to this observation, taken from *Cancer as a Turning Point*:

> Over and over again I have seen one of two things happen when the total environment of the person with cancer is mobilized for life, and his or her inner ecology is thereby changed in a positive way. For some, the patient's life is prolonged, not in an arbitrary way, but in order that there may be more experience of the self . . . and the recognition— and often fulfillment—of dreams. And then there were the genuine miracles—not magic, but dedicated hard work which made the cancer a turning point in the person's life rather than a sign of its ending.

There are no guarantees, but when we let cancer—or any other disease—become a psychospiritual turning point rather than the start of a downward spiral, we give mind and body a better chance to get well. And even if we don't get physically better, counting our days "rightly, that we may acquire a heart of wisdom," to use an older translation from the Jewish Publication Society, is still the essence of healing beyond cure. Our days may be fewer in number, but their richness is what matters.

Dr. LeShan's entire approach to treating people with cancer is to help them unearth not what is wrong with them but what is right with them. He facilitates a process in which the newly diagnosed patient discovers his or her own "unique ways of being, relating, and creating." This translates as daily endeavors that yield zest and purpose from morning to night. According to Dr. LeShan, when patients find and activate their will to live, their immune systems get the message, "Keep on fighting."

When it comes to illness, the valiant battles lost bring no less honor and dignity than those that are won.

Psalm 90 turns our temporal conception of life upside down. "For in Your sight a thousand years are like yesterday that has past." From our point of view, a thousand years is a vast stretch of time; we celebrate the new millennium as a major historical event. But from God's point of view, a thousand years represents a quick flash, "like a watch of the night."

Life is but a "sigh," a short melancholic exhalation. "The span of our life is seventy years, or, given the strength, eighty years; but the best of them are trouble and sorrow. They pass by speedily, and we fly away." Many of us harbor the quasi-conscious belief that our sentient lives will go on forever. But we need a sense of our own mortality, lest we miss out on the gravity and opportunity in each hour, each day.

The key verse, instructing us to count our days rightly, is mirrored in a beautiful passage in Psalm 39:

> *Tell me, O Lord, what my term is,*
> *what is the measure of my days. . . .*
> *Man walks about as a mere shadow;*
> *mere futility is his hustle and bustle. . . .*
> *What, then, can I count on, O Lord?*

Scientist and clinician Jerome Groopman, M.D., who specializes in cancer and AIDS, has written an alternately heartbreaking and inspiring book about his encounters with patients with life-threatening disease. The book is titled, after the above verse, *The Measure of Our Days*. After citing this passage in his prologue, Dr. Groopman reveals the turning point in his own life: As a second-year medical student at Columbia University, he received a call in the middle of the night from his mother, informing him that his father, "the person I admired most in the world, who had centered and guided my life," had had a massive heart attack. Dr. Groopman arrived at the hospital in time to witness his father's demise. "He died before his time, and without time—time for him, his family, and his friends to prepare for his passing."

"The experience explains in part my powerful commitment to care for patients and their loved ones in a way that my father and my family were not cared for—with genuine compassion and scientific excellence," writes Dr. Groopman. "And it provides a very personal point of reference for why I find the time before death so precious, so worth fighting for."

Would that more physicians and patients could, together, work with the same passion and perseverance to make worthwhile every hour of every day that is granted to them. At the end of *The Measure of Our Days*, Dr. Groopman tells the story of his own dear friend's recovery from lymphoma and, later, treatment-related leukemia, with prolonged regimens of toxic chemotherapy and a bone marrow transplant. His friend ultimately survived, and on the book's final page, Dr. Groopman is reminded of the key verses in Psalm 90, which are recited during the Sabbath and at the beginning of *yizkor*, the Jewish service of remembrance of loved ones lost. "This time," writes Dr. Groopman, "the words spoke to me not of loss but of gain."

The Psalm that instructs us to "count our days rightly" reminds us that each day offers the prospect of renewal. "You engulf men in sleep; at daybreak they are like grass that renews itself; at daybreak it flourishes anew . . . " And what does the Psalmist ask of God? "Satisfy us at daybreak with Your steadfast love." While life may be brief, God's love enables us to "sing for joy all our days," no matter their number.

PSALM 103

◆ ◆ ◆

TO RECOGNIZE THE GOD
OF COMPASSION

The Lord is compassionate and gracious,

slow to anger,

abounding in steadfast love.

TO RECOGNIZE THE GOD
OF COMPASSION

PSALM 103

◆ ◆ ◆

Bless the Lord, O my soul,
  all my being, His holy name.
Bless the Lord, O my soul
  and do not forget all His bounties.
He forgives all your sins,
  heals all your diseases.
He redeems your life from the Pit,
  surrounds you with steadfast love and mercy.
He satisfies you with good things in the prime of
    life,
  so that your youth is renewed like the eagle's.

The Lord executes righteous acts
  and judgments for all who are wronged.
He made known His ways to Moses,
  His deeds to the children of Israel.

The Lord is compassionate and gracious,
    slow to anger, abounding in steadfast love. . . .
He has not dealt with us according to our sins,
    nor has He requited us according to our iniquities.
For as the heavens are high above the earth,
    so great is His steadfast love toward those who
        fear Him.
As east is far from west,
    so far has He removed our sins from us.
As a father has compassion for his children,
    so the Lord has compassion for those who fear
        Him.
For He knows how we are formed;
    He is mindful that we are dust.

Man, his days are like those of grass;
    he blooms like a flower in the field;
    a wind passes by and it is no more,
    its own place no longer knows it.
But the Lord's steadfast love is for all eternity
    toward those who fear Him, . . .

Bless the Lord, O His angels,
    mighty creatures who do His bidding,
    ever obedient to His bidding;
    bless the Lord, all His hosts,
    His servants who do His will;
    bless the Lord, all His works,
    through the length and breadth of His realm;
    bless the Lord, O my soul.

The God of compassion is nowhere more evident than in this lyrical Psalm. He "forgives all your sins" and "surrounds you with steadfast love and mercy." Most important, He does not condition His steadfast love on whether or how you have sinned.

This has special resonance for those of us afflicted with illness. The God of compassion who "heals all [our] diseases" also does not "[deal] with us according to our sins." This God, "abounding in steadfast love," would not punish us for misdeeds by striking us down with life-threatening diseases. All of us have committed mistakes and transgressions; it is not in God's cosmic blueprint to render punishment by inflicting illness. Why would a merciful God smite a person who has engaged in some wrongdoing but has otherwise lived an exemplary life? Aren't most of our sick friends or family members basically good human beings with flaws? Aren't we the same? If our spiritual philosophy is centered on a spiteful Deity, we need to go deeper in our effort to arrive at a mature understanding of God.

Too often, when we're sick, we ask ourselves the question, "Why is God punishing me? I must have done something to deserve this." We search for reasons to blame ourselves, reasons why we're being condemned to suffer. I recall a professor at City College in New York City once saying, "When I get sick, I know that God is punishing me." I didn't believe that for a second, but at City College in the mid-1940s, we didn't tell our professors that they didn't know what they were talking about. Yet it's a common misconception, one worth questioning and ultimately replacing.

Those of us who punish ourselves over an illness would do well to remember these two verses from Psalm 103: "The Lord is compassionate and gracious, slow to anger, abounding in steadfast love. . . . He has not dealt with us according to our sins, nor has He requited us according to our iniquities."

While God's wrath certainly appears in the Bible and the Book of Psalms, we ought to redefine our concept of an angry God. We can honor the Bible's conception without having to posit a harshly punitive God, especially since biblical references to God's loving-kindness far outnumber mentions of His wrath. One way to understand God's anger as delineated in the Bible is that it's the basis for our moral compass.

God sounds a piercing siren when we are engaged—or about to engage—in conduct that is evil or corrupt, because it harms others, shreds the social fabric, or otherwise flouts ethical precepts. A compassionate God wants us to *hear* His rebuke over harmful behavior so that we don't diminish ourselves and hurt the people in our midst. That rebuke, internalized, is a healthy part of our psyches: the conscience. But when we punish ourselves with cruel criticisms over old or imagined misdeeds, we are not doing God's bidding. Psychologists call this unhealthy shame, and it has nothing to do with the development of a moral conscience. If anything, unhealthy shame only makes us dreadfully insecure and overly self-involved.

Where does the notion of a compassionate God originate? In Exodus, the second of the Five Books of Moses, the story is told of Moses' return from Mount Sinai with the stone tablets containing the Ten Commandments. After seeing the Israelites worshipping a golden calf, a reversion to the pagan practices that God had forbidden, Moses destroyed the tablets in a fit of rage. God then instructed Moses to return to Mount Sinai with two newly carved tablets of stone upon which the Ten Commandments would again be inscribed. When Moses went back up Mount Sinai, God "came down in a cloud" and made a series of startling proclamations, which are recorded in Exodus 34.

Psalm 103 is a virtual meditation on God's proclamations in Exodus 34. They read, in part: "The Lord! The

Lord! a God compassionate and gracious, slow to anger, abounding in kindness and faithfulness, extending kindness to the thousandth generation, forgiving iniquity, transgression, and sin. . . . " The central theme of Psalm 103 is derived from this biblical passage, words that people and families struggling with illness can take to heart.

These same words, central to the Jewish liturgy, are spoken during the pilgrimage festivals (Passover, Shavuot, and Sukkot), and the High Holidays (Rosh Hashanah and Yom Kippur). The liturgists made sure that people recognized the God of mercy on every important occasion during which they gathered for repentance or contemplation.

The Psalm is full of hope and a life-affirming dynamism. "He satisfies you with good things in the prime of life, so that your youth is renewed like the eagle's." (In the *Soncino Books of the Bible* translation, "prime of life" is "old age.") Whether you read *prime of life* to mean 40, 80, or somewhere in between, it's the time when most of us grapple with illness and strive for healing. Why the image of the eagle? As the great 11th-century Jewish scholar Rashi notes in his biblical commentary, "the eagle grows new feathers in the place of old, and it lives to a great age and yet retains its vitality." With faith in a merciful God, the possibilities of renewal—even rejuvenation—are bountiful.

Belief in a God of loving-kindness enables us to make our way in the world with hope, confidence, and open hearts. This is eloquently expressed by Thomas Traherne, the 17th-century English poet, in a passage quoted in Aldous Huxley's classic *The Perennial Philosophy*:

> Till your spirit filleth the whole world, and the stars are your jewels; till you are as familiar with the ways of God in all ages as with your walk and table; till you are intimately acquainted with that shady nothing out of which the world was made; till you love men so as to desire their happiness with a thirst equal to the zeal of your own; till you delight in God for being good to all; you never enjoy the world.

Scholars have suggested that the Book of Psalms contains the purest odes to the God of compassion. In his book *God: A Biography*, Jack Miles, a former Jesuit trained in religious studies, makes this very point. Referring to the Psalms, Miles writes, "their praise certainly goes disproportionately to *sedeq* and *hesed*, God's righteousness and his steadfast love, rather than to his prowess in battle or his bounty."

People who consciously or unconsciously believe in a vengeful God will either blame themselves for an illness

("God is punishing me") or blame God ("What kind of ter-rible God could do this?"). As a rabbi, I have tried to help many anguished people and their families who have fallen into this way of thinking and feeling. Dealing with illness, fear, and grief is hard enough; an overlay of shame and rage only makes it harder. Such misconceptions about God come out of pain, not clarity. They also derive, typically, from religious ideas inculcated early in life, ideas that resurface when illness or tragedy strikes.

Perhaps we were taught in our early religious training that a personal God keeps tabs on our good and bad deeds, that He wreaks vengeance for every one of our sins. Or maybe our parents were strict disciplinarians who meted out severe punishments, and we grew up believing that the Almighty must reflect our parents' ways. As a result, we ei-ther developed a view of God as an avenger or gave up on God altogether because we never saw Him as a source of wisdom or loving-kindness.

When a crisis hits and we're scared and spiritually adrift, we are liable to search for the God in Whom we can trust. Given our upbringings, we may discover one of two things: Either He is not there at all, or He surfaces as a voice of condemnation, one that makes us cringe or lash out in fury.

When this occurs, we can consciously choose to transform our religious and spiritual mindsets. We can question the nature of the God we were instructed to believe in. We can develop a mature understanding of God based no longer on the fears or magical thinking of childhood. We can bring to this inquiry our own profoundly personal beliefs about ourselves, our fellow men and women, and the nature of the universe.

Our concept of the Absolute may stray from the doctrines of the religion in which we were raised. For instance, some of us cannot accept the notion of a personal God, but we believe in God as a "force" nonetheless. We must honor our beliefs, using our heads and hearts to arrive at spiritual principles and practices that make sense to us. But we can look to the Psalms and other biblical texts to find a God, however conceptualized, of limitless mercy. ("The Lord's steadfast love is for all eternity.") We can be inspired by the realization that the texts of the world's great religions contain ample evidence of God's unconditional love and forgiveness.

We can find contradictory ideas and images in the canons of every major religion, which only underscores the fact that each of us must choose what to believe. We must interpret and gain from these texts what *we* find valuable—that which guides our conscience and speaks to our hearts. In my experience, people in crisis need to recognize a God of compassion, not a strict father or a magical savior. They need to know that, whatever happens to them, they will be neither abandoned nor judged harshly but accompanied with every breath by a higher power of infinite love and acceptance.

Such a God offers hope for a full recovery, for He is a veritable bastion of moral and physical strength. If we are not physically healed, the same God remains a fount of strength, to live every moment with fullness, meaning, and loving intent.

Psalm 68

◆　◆　◆

TO SHARE OUR BURDENS
WITH GOD

Blessed is the Lord.

Day by day He bears

our burden,

God, our deliverance.

To Share Our Burdens
with God

Psalm 68

◆ ◆ ◆

. . . Sing to God, chant hymns to His name;
*   extol Him who rides the clouds;*
*   the Lord is His name.*
Exult in His presence—
*   the father of orphans, the champion of widows,*
*   God, in His holy habitation. . . .*

Blessed is the Lord.
Day by day He bears our burden,
*   God, our deliverance.*
God is for us a God of deliverance;
*   God the Lord provides an escape from*
*   death. . . .*

The burdens of illness are ones that we will inevitably have to bear. It's likely that we will contend with the aches and anxieties, the side effects of treatment, the daily tensions that give way to nightly shudders. And during our travails, the mundane problems don't go away. Financial strains, familial conflicts, and troubles at work tend to layer on top of the physical and emotional trials of disease.

"Illness is the night side of life, a more onerous citizenship," writes Susan Sontag in *Illness as Metaphor*. "Everyone who is born holds dual citizenship, in the kingdom of the well and in the kingdom of the sick. Although we all prefer to use only the good passport, sooner or later each of us is obliged, for at least a spell, to identify ourselves as citizens of that other place."

Once we've passed into "the kingdom of the sick," we wonder how we can navigate this unfamiliar, often threatening terrain. On one level, the answer is fairly obvious: Get the best medical care and the strongest support from loved ones. This is critical, no doubt. But our "other" citizenship is indeed onerous, with moments of terror and bewilderment that defy rational solutions. Doctors may not have all the answers; rarely can they offer guarantees like those proffered by car salesmen and insurance brokers. The loving support of family members is essential, but our caretakers have their emotional and physical limitations. And there may be moments, in that other country, when we are alone, as if stranded on an island in the dark, with no seeming escape from isolation and no one to share our predicament.

Who, then, will bear our burdens?

"Blessed is the Lord. Day by day He bears our burden, God, our deliverance." That is the answer offered by Psalm 68. I recommend this particular verse to people in trouble, and I even dare to say that God *shares* our burdens, since I believe that we can share our burdens with God. I refer to both meanings of the word *share*: We communicate our burdens to the Lord, and we cooperate in taking responsibility for them.

We communicate our burdens to God through the language of prayer. When our hope is slipping and there is nothing left to do about our circumstances, we can turn, in our most private moments, to the Absolute. A great Hasidic rabbi, Nachman of Bratzlav, once said that every person needs time to be alone, by himself, for contemplation and prayer. It may be late at night, before sleep, when the forces competing for our attention have gone into retreat and we can turn inward. We look back on the day, asking ourselves what we've experienced and what we need to persevere and grow through our difficulties. Disquiet and puzzlement may arise, prompting us to turn directly to God with our hardships. We should feel free to pray in any way, using any language or phrasing, that brings us closer to God.

Some of us wish to pray for complete recovery, for freedom from physical and spiritual suffering. While no one should demur from asking God to relieve his or her anguish, I often suggest that people focus their prayers a bit differently—that is, simply, to ask God for the courage and wisdom to face whatever will come. Rather than request that everything go well, we can petition God's help to secure the inner and outer resources to fight the fight, accept our losses, and build on our progress.

Praying for the strength to deal with whatever transpires is a powerful way to share our burdens with God. When we petition God for recovery and we experience setbacks, we may become disillusioned. Such disenchantment with God is understandable, but it's also a reversion to the old notion of a paternalistic God who grants or denies requests based on a set of cosmic criteria. Within that magical mindset, when our illnesses worsen, we assume that we either haven't been good enough or haven't prayed hard or well enough.

Praying for courage, wisdom, and support acknowledges God as the ground of creation rather than as the heavenly puppeteer. It also helps us avoid disillusionment, a form of spiritual "throwing in the towel" that can lead to despair. We need to preserve our relationships with God; we will need Him for the tough times ahead and even for the good times, since God's presence helps us to savor every moment of well-being.

Some people who petition God for recovery or wellness manage to avoid disillusionment. When they suffer setbacks, they don't blame themselves, and they don't blame God. They maintain a balance between seeking and acceptance, shifting between the "make it happen" and "let it be" forms of prayer. Abraham Joshua Heschel, who wrote eloquently about the varieties of prayer, captured this balance in his book *Moral Grandeur and Spiritual Audacity*:

The main ends of prayer are to move God, to let Him participate in our lives, and to interest ourselves in Him. What is the meaning of praise if not to make His concern our own? Worship is an act of inner agreement with God. We can only petition Him for things we need when we are sure of His sympathy for us. To praise is to feel God's concern; to petition is to let Him feel our concern. In prayer we establish a living contract with God, between our concern and His will, between despair and promise, want and abundance. We affirm our adherence by invoking His love.

If we can manage such a balance, we will be able to up-hold or even deepen our faith as we petition God. If we can't, then asking God for wisdom and courage—or just using prayer to move closer in our consciousness to God—can at least ground us in a sustainable spirituality.

We may reach a breaking point in our struggle with ill-ness when we recognize that we can't control every facet of the fight. We've obtained the best medical care and pro-cured the support of loved ones. Will the disease remit? Will we get well? It's time to turn to God for help and hope.

The New Age and 12-step recovery movements talk of "surrender" or "turning it over" to God. I think that these concepts have some validity, but we must be a bit careful here.

The term *surrender* suggests that we let God take care of us. That strikes me as a shade too passive and helpless. In the healing endeavor, we need a partnership with God. We can pursue medical options and activate the curative ca-pabilities within ourselves. We can mobilize those powers through meditation and prayer, even by visualizing our bodies' defenses fending off disease agents. We might call this active faith, as opposed to passive faith in which we ask God to do the work.

In one study, researcher Lydia Temoshok, Ph.D., of the University of California, San Francisco, discovered that melanoma patients who exhibited passive faith, saying "It's in God's hands" or "It's in the doctor's hands," had more progressive disease than those who took a more active role in their recovery. Many active patients used prayer or meditation for spiritual support, but not from a position of helplessness. "I pray," said one of Dr. Temoshok's active patients, a middle-aged man diagnosed with a potentially lethal melanoma. "I believe in God. I believe in life after death. Naturally, I've been frightened. But I have a strong element of hope. I don't want to die right now. I'm using all my resources and faith and knowledge."

We can recognize that we have little control over certain aspects of our recovery without becoming passive in our efforts to control what we can. Throughout, we can petition God's help to buttress all our resources, external and internal. We might ask God to help us find inner peace when we hit a "wall," a juncture in our struggle with illness at which we have no control, such as when we await the results of a crucial diagnostic test. That's why I alter the interpretation of the verse in Psalm 68 to "Blessed is the Lord, who day by day shares our burden."

People diagnosed with severe illnesses and those who

have suffered searing losses have said to me, "It's God's will." I always beg to differ. I don't think it's God's will that children get cancer, that parents die of diseases when their children are still young, or that anyone experience a prolonged and painful death. I believe that God's original blueprint makes such occurrences all but inevitable; we are vulnerable, mortal beings. But it's also God's plan that men and women resist and overcome disastrous diseases. Human beings have been granted virtually limitless intellectual faculties so that we can, as time unfolds, master diseases and live longer, healthier lives. Isn't that what history has taught us?

When I was a rabbi in Quincy, Massachusetts, in the early 1950s, there was a virtual epidemic of polio in our state. At the time, a lovely young woman in my congregation, Marjorie, was stricken with polio. When she was 18, one of her legs became paralyzed from the disease. One year later, Jonas Salk perfected his polio vaccine, and this prevalent, crippling disease was wiped out. Did God *want* people like Marjorie to be struck down, and did He then reverse His decision in order to protect people? Why would God have given us the gifts to defeat disease if He wished to use illness as a punishment and health as a reward?

If we review the history of medicine and project our understanding into the future, God's plan becomes clear: It's not for us to develop a medical route to immortality but rather to strive—and succeed—in developing cures for diseases that cut down people's lives in their prime and cause immense suffering. A century ago, who would have imagined that we would defeat polio and smallpox, cure half of all cancers, and devise methods to prevent and cure heart disease? While AIDS has not been conquered, for vast numbers it is now a chronic, manageable disease. Where will we be a century from now? God's miracles are delivered through the heads, hearts, and hands of men and women.

We are even learning that physical regeneration can be induced by natural medicines, derived from plants that sprout from the earth, and by our own inner resources, the body's healing defenses reinforced by a calm mind and a steadfast heart. What does that tell us about God's design for health and healing?

From my perspective, God suffers when our anguish is most profound. He has created a world in which mortal beings have free will; we struggle, endure, triumph, wither, and move to the next level, whatever that may be. God may be closer to a compassionate witness than to an omnipotent wizard. He is saddened when we are saddened, outraged when we are outraged, present when we need

His presence. Viewed this way, when we experience tragic losses, we realize that it would be as inappropriate to rage at God as it would be to rage at our dearest friends, the ones who stand by our sides through our lowest moments.

In the Jewish tradition, life is holy, and we are charged with the sacred responsibility to value and protect life. We are taught to focus our concerns on making this world a better place for all sentient beings. But most Jews and Jewish scholars believe that the soul is not extinguished when life leaves the body. The soul lives on, and although there are wide disagreements about the soul's precise fate, one belief is that the soul continues its growth and learning process—"studying," if you will—this time with the ultimate Teacher.

The Psalmist refers to the soul's fate when he intones, "God is for us a God of deliverance; God the Lord provides an escape from death." None of us escapes physical death, but the Psalmist suggests that our souls meet God in the hereafter. For some of us, it's hard to visualize or grasp what this means, but even though it's hard to live with confusion, we can live with mystery.

PSALM 71

◆ ◆ ◆

TO FORGE HEALTH
AND HEALING AS WE AGE

Do not cast me off in old age;

when my strength fails,

do not forsake me!

TO FORGE HEALTH
AND HEALING AS WE AGE

PSALM 71

$$\blacklozenge \quad \blacklozenge \quad \blacklozenge$$

I seek refuge in You, O Lord;
  may I never be disappointed.
As You are beneficent, save me and rescue me;
  incline Your ear to me and deliver me.
Be a sheltering rock for me to which I may
    always repair;
  decree my deliverance,
  for You are my rock and my fortress. . . .
For You are my hope,
  O Lord God,
  my trust from my youth.
While yet unborn, I depended on You;
  in the womb of my mother, You were my
    support;
  I sing Your praises always.
I have become an example for many,
  since You are my mighty refuge.

My mouth is full of praise to You,
   glorifying You all day long.
Do not cast me off in old age;
   when my strength fails, do not forsake me! . . .

I come with praise of Your mighty acts, O Lord
      God;
   I celebrate Your beneficence, Yours alone.
You have let me experience it, God, from my
      youth;
   until now I have proclaimed Your wondrous
     deeds,
   and even in hoary old age do not forsake me,
     God,
   until I proclaim Your strength to the next
     generation,
   Your mighty acts, to all who are to come,
   Your beneficence, high as the heavens, O
     God,
   You who have done great things;
   O God, who is Your peer! . . .
You will grant me much greatness,
   You will turn and comfort me.
Then I will acclaim You to the music of the lyre
   for Your faithfulness, O my God;
   I will sing a hymn to You with a harp,
   O Holy One of Israel.
My lips shall be jubilant, as I sing a hymn to You,
   my whole being, which You have redeemed. . . .

Aging and illness go hand in hand, and now that medical technology is enabling us to live longer, we are facing the problem of living *well* despite the inevitable disorders and disabilities. As we age, we typically must endure more health crises, and we wonder how we will be able to remain self-sustaining and independent. We don't want to become wholly dependent on our children or other relatives or friends. We want to retain not only our health but also our self-esteem, productivity, creativity, and dignity.

So, managing our aging becomes a tall order. From where will we draw our strength? The crux of Psalm 71 is that we can turn to God for sustenance and deeper meaning as we age. The climax of the Psalm is a plea: "Do not cast me off in old age; when my strength fails, do not forsake me!" The end of the Psalm is an answer to that plea: "You will grant me much greatness, You will turn and comfort me."

The most poignant verse, "Do not cast [us] off in old age, when [our] strength fails," is sung three times during the most sacred Jewish holiday, Yom Kippur, when the ark containing the Torah (the scroll of the Five Books of Moses) is opened. Jews around the world have often cried when singing these words, which seem to stir that universal anxiety about aging, the fear not only of incapacity and dependency but also of facing the reality of unfulfilled dreams.

The beauty and gravity of this Psalm lie in its evocation of our yearning to live our twilight years with purpose, energy, and self-respect. At the same time, the Psalm answers that yearning with a rousing expression of faith in the form of a celebratory hymn to God the redeemer.

Some of us don't find our spiritual connection until we are older, after a lifetime of questioning, loss, and change has enabled us to find our own unique path to God. Lois, a dear friend, lived most of her lifetime alienated from Judaism, the religion in which she was raised. While she always believed in God, she never found a route to actualize her belief, to make it real, to weave it into the fabric of her life. As a teenager and young woman, she had rebelled against what she experienced as her parent's rigid approach to Judaism, and for most of the rest of her life, she had very few ties to religion.

Lois's adulthood was a hard one with much disappointment and loss, including the sudden, untimely death of her first husband when he was in his forties. Her difficulties did not make it easier for Lois to develop a clear-eyed spiritual life; if anything, they prompted even more uncertainty about God and religion. A number of years after the death of her first husband, Lois remarried. When she was in her sixties, she retired from her job as a nurse, and she and her husband, Mel, moved from the Northeast to southern Florida. Only then did Lois begin in earnest to search for a spiritual and religious life that could fill her later years with a sense of relatedness to others and to God.

Lois began attending services at a local synagogue and struck up a relationship with the rabbi there. Lois is an extremely bright woman, and she appreciated what he had to offer and began to reconnect with Jewish rituals of prayer and observance. Her spiritual hunger had been strong, and it was finally sated, at least to some extent.

Lois's newfound religious affiliation helped her to deal with the onset of serious heart disease. After undergoing heart bypass surgery, she also joined a meditation and dietary program for heart health, where she befriended Kathy, a fellow member of the group. When Kathy died, her daughter asked Lois if she would speak at the funeral, which would take place in a church. Lois was moved by the request, and she called to ask me whether it would be appropriate to ask the mourners to stand while she said kaddish, the prayer that Jews recite for loved ones who have departed. (Kaddish affirms our faith in God at the time when it is most difficult to do so.) I said that I thought it would be a lovely gesture. Shortly after the funeral, Lois received a letter from Kathy's daughter thanking her for the beautiful tribute. For Lois, sharing this time-honored ritual enabled her to memorialize her friend *and* affirm the faith that she had finally found in her twilight years.

When Lois was in her early seventies, her husband, Mel, died. Lois was fortunate to have already found a spiritual connection and a supportive spiritual community, since they helped her to cope surprisingly well with her loss. I doubt whether Lois would have had the same strength and perspective in the aftermath of Mel's death had she not genuinely felt that she could turn to God in her loneliness and sorrow. In the years since, her spirit has remained strong, despite her loss and other hard times. Lois's spiritual practice and participation in her religious community have become enduring parts of her life. It is a life of dignity and purpose.

Too much of the pain of aging results from our society's lack of regard for its elders. In her book *Another Country*, Mary Pipher, Ph.D., writes:

We are in a new world with no real prototypes for dealing with all these aging people. Medicine has both helped and complicated our situation. Many people live longer and healthier lives. But unhealthy people live longer, too. We have thousands of citizens who lie comatose in long-term health-care facilities. Bodies last longer than brains, support systems, or savings accounts. We don't have the resources, the rituals, or the institutions to make our old feel like elders.

The physical aches of aging are difficult enough, but the psychological and spiritual aches are perhaps harder—and they make the physical ones worse. In his famous essay "The Eight Ages of Man," psychologist Erik Erikson speaks of the final stage of life as characterized by a struggle between "ego integrity" and despair. "Despair expresses the feeling that the time is now short, too short for the attempt to start another life and to try alternate roads to integrity."

But despair is not inevitable. Even if it's too late to "start another life," it is never too late to try alternate roads to integrity. Though society should do more to make aging a positive experience, turning to God through meditation and prayer is one of the most empowering ways that we can transform our own experience of aging.

Mind-body scientist George F. Solomon, M.D., professor emeritus at the University of California, Los Angeles, has studied the healthy elderly, looking for answers to the question "What keeps them so healthy?" He developed a profile of the healthy elderly person, who was likely to be a "good coper," a "problem solver," a "help seeker," and an "optimist" who remained socially connected and vitally involved in activities that kept his or her passions alive.

Psalm 71, which captures the longing for comfort and joy as we age, unfolds as the sacred story of a life, especially in the middle verses. The Psalmist depends on God through each developmental stage: "While yet unborn, I depended on You; in the womb of my mother, You were my support." "For You are my hope . . . my trust from my youth." "Even in hoary old age do not forsake me, God."

God does not forsake us as we age. But we can meet Him halfway, moving to Him through prayer, through service to humankind, and through forms of tender self-care that lift us up despite our hardships and ailments.

We may ask ourselves existential questions, such as "Has my life mattered?" "Have I made a difference?" "Will anybody remember me when I'm gone?" Somerset Maugham once said, "All my life I have believed in 'later.' But there is no 'later' now." These are hard questions and tough realizations, but with God there is always the potential for light, experienced in mindful moments of pleasure, time with family, or quiet contemplation. If we are physically able, then remaining active, not only through exercise but also through meaningful work or creative pursuits, keeps us vibrant in body and soul.

Prayer is not another in a line of anti-aging approaches. I don't think that we should *fight* the aging process as if it were a shameful and depressing final chapter to be avoided at all costs. Rather, we can grow into our aging, accepting the inevitable changes while defying negative connotations such as *decline* and *deterioration*. We may slow aspects of aging with medicine, nutrition, and spiritual pursuits, but that's different from waging war on a natural process.

Many years ago, an elderly man named Aaron taught the bar and bat mitzvah students at our synagogue. Aaron was unfailingly kind, gentle, and thoughtful with our children, who were not always delighted by the rather arduous preparations for the service. As he got older, Aaron could no longer make it to the temple, so he requested that he continue teaching the children by phone. When he reached his nineties, he was not as sharp in his phone lessons, and some of the children became impatient.

Aaron's adult children were members of our congregation, and, knowing that their father was having trouble,
they requested a private talk with me. They asked if they
could pay Aaron's salary so that he could continue to
teach, but they wanted it to appear as though his salary
were still coming from the temple. I agreed, and we informed the young students that they could choose
whether to continue being taught by Aaron, explaining
that it was a mitzvah—a good deed—to help an elderly
person retain his dignity. About half of the children chose
to stick with Aaron. He continued teaching for another 6
months before he died.

Afterward, Aaron's son and daughter moved away from
our community, but they returned for frequent visits, and
they would always thank me for helping their father retain
his dignity and purpose until the end of his life. In turn, I
would remind them that in making their request, they fulfilled the teaching of a great midrash, or story, which says,
"When we welcome and honor an older person, it is as if
we have welcomed and honored the Shechinah itself—the
Divine Presence."

As we age, we can help ourselves deal with present-day
infirmities and disappointments by talking about them.
But we can also share our hopes and achievements, our

moments of regret and acts of goodness, our sad and rapturous memories. As loved ones of the aging, we can simply be there to listen—the highest act of caring.

As our bodies begin to play tricks with us, we search for meaning that transcends the body. One road to meaning as we age is to "proclaim [God's] strength to the next generation." In so doing, we not only pass a torch but also remind ourselves of our own spiritual roots, our own gratitude for the goodness in life and God's ultimate deliverance. Thus, appropriately, the final verses of Psalm 71 are filled with joy: "My lips shall be jubilant, as I sing a hymn to You, my whole being, which You have redeemed."

ACCEPTANCE AND RECOVERY

PSALM 118

◆ ◆ ◆

TO AFFIRM
AND CELEBRATE LIFE

I shall not die but live

and proclaim the

works of the Lord.

TO AFFIRM
AND CELEBRATE LIFE

PSALM 118

—— ◆ ◆ ◆ ——

. . . In distress I called on the Lord;
  the Lord answered me and brought me relief.
The Lord is on my side,
  I have no fear;
  what can man do to me?
With the Lord on my side as my helper,
  I will see the downfall of my foes.

It is better to take refuge in the Lord
  than to trust in mortals;
  it is better to take refuge in the Lord
  than to trust in the great. . . .

The Lord is my strength and might;
  He has become my deliverance.
The tents of the righteous resound with joyous
  shouts of deliverance,

*"The right hand of the Lord is
    triumphant! . . ."*

*I shall not die but live
    and proclaim the works of the Lord. . . .*

*Open the gates of victory for me
    that I may enter them and praise the Lord.
This is the gateway to the Lord—
    the victorious shall enter through it.*

*I praise You, for You have answered me,
    and have become my deliverance.
The stone that the builders rejected
    has become the chief cornerstone.
This is the Lord's doing;
    it is marvelous in our sight.
This is the day that the Lord has made—
    let us exult and rejoice on it. . . .*

There are times in the course of an illness when we want to give up the fight. We're tired of the tests, the fear, the treatments, the hospital food, the physical pain, the uncertainty about our prognosis. It's entirely understandable and no sign of a character deficiency on our part when we feel hopeless, exhausted, and resigned. But if we never climb out of hopelessness, if we are unable to reclaim our desire for life, our emotional and physical recovery becomes vastly more difficult. The research evidence is building that people with cancer, heart disease, and other diseases may have more trouble getting well—and staying well—once they lapse into chronic depression and despair.

The answer, according to health psychologists, is not to try to remain cheerful at all costs, planting smiles on our faces to please loved ones or to live up to a fantasized ideal about the mind-body road to health. The best approach is to allow ourselves to feel hopeless but to share those feelings so that they don't fester inside. When we work through vexing emotions, turning to others for solace and support, the feelings themselves change character. They shift and shuttle back and forth, from despair to joie de vivre, from pessimism to optimism, from surrender to resistance. This "cycling" seems to be the most natural, even healthy, response to the painful vicissitudes of serious illness.

Sharing this cycle with supportive friends can strengthen our recovery and even lengthen our lives, as studies of heart disease and cancer patients in group therapy have shown. Many of us, however, get stuck in hopelessness and despair. The way to cycle out of anguish is to get help. We must have the courage to ask our loved ones, doctors, counselors, therapists, and clergypeople for practical and emotional support. Crying on the shoulder of someone who cares may seem like a trite prescription, but in the right circumstances, it is powerful medicine.

But there is another way to get help, and that is from the God of our faith. Among the most exultant and optimistic of all the Psalms, Psalm 118 celebrates God's presence in our lives as the fount of our fighting spirit. (It is one the six Psalms of Praise, known collectively as Hallel, that Jews pray on the festival holidays.) Some verses veritably sing with praise for God's intervention as helper and savior: "The Lord is my strength and might; He has become my deliverance. The tents of the righteous resound with joyous shouts of deliverance, 'The right hand of the Lord is triumphant!'"

We might wonder: If psychological studies have shown that medical patients are emotionally and physically strengthened by the support of loved ones and professionals, why do they need God? Psalm 118 offers the clearest response: "It is better to take refuge in the Lord than to trust in mortals; it is better to take refuge in the Lord than to trust in the great."

I don't interpret this verse to mean that mortals and even the "great" ones—doctors, therapists, and so on—are never to be trusted. Rather, it acknowledges that members of our support system have feet of clay.

Doctors are not perfect. They may make wrong medical decisions, and they frequently fall short in giving patients the moral and emotional support that they need. The managed-care system pressures them to limit their visits with patients to egg-timer proportions, so it's not all their fault. Therapists, priests, rabbis, and other pastoral counselors are not available round the clock, and they don't always say or do just the right thing. Alternative medicine practitioners have many prescriptions, but they don't always work. Even the most steadfast family members and friends are likely to fail us at one time or another.

"It is better to take refuge in the Lord" suggests that there is *never* a time when we cannot place our trust in God. God's steadfastness complements the Godlike but fallible ministrations of the human beings in our midst, the caring doctors, nurses, counselors, wives, husbands, siblings, parents, children, and dear friends. It also suggests that we take refuge in the Lord whenever we are stuck in despair, unable to fight through the thicket of conflicting and agonizing emotions about our illnesses. In moments when no human hand can lead us out of the trap of resignation, God is there, with His answers, His deliverance.

When we worry that an illness has us in its grasp, there is always this verse: "I shall not die but live and proclaim the works of the Lord." One cannot find a more stirring cry of fighting spirit in the entire Psalter. "I shall not die but live" is the passionate, even defiant shout of the person whose intent is to resist his or her demise with every available ounce of energy and resolve.

I never tell a person with a life-threatening disease to cultivate a fighting spirit on the grounds that it will surely lead to recovery. I've seen too many optimistic fighters with cancer, AIDS, or heart disease who have still succumbed (though they won the fight for a fuller, richer life during their remaining time).

But several studies suggest that fighting spirit somehow transmutes in the body to a stronger defense against disease. In his seminal research, Steven Greer, M.D., of the Royal Marsden Hospital in London found that breast cancer patients who evidenced fighting spirit were more than twice as likely to be alive 15 years after their diagnosis than patients who felt helpless and hopeless. Nothing could sum up the attitude of those women with fighting spirit better than the phrase "I shall not die but live."

And what do we do with the life that we've gained in the fight? "Proclaim the works of the Lord," says Psalm 118. Elena Kanter, a rabbi at Temple Beth El in Birmingham, Alabama, wrote an inspiring piece in the periodical *Sh'ma*, about her own struggle with cancer in which she described how this very verse was a source of wisdom and conviction:

The morning after I received the news that I had cancer and that I was going to have surgery, I went to shul [synagogue]. It was Shemini Atzeret [a festival], and I did what I always do on Shemini Atzeret, which is go to shul. Concentration was hard because there were so many thoughts and feelings—everything coming at once, hard to organize or make any coherence out of the whole mishmash.

But I got to Hallel, the special Psalms of praise we add on holidays . . . I reached the verse that says . . . "I shall not die but live, and I will tell of the works of the Lord"—or loosely translated, "I will tell stories about God." As I read that verse, I knew at that moment that it expressed the content of my heart. I wasn't going to die, I was going to live and I was going to live to tell about God. Walking into the synagogue that morning, I wasn't thinking of that verse. But when I read it that morning in shul, it helped me to express what I was feeling, the determination that I was going to live and not die.

Rabbi Kanter was going to live *to tell about God*. In a sense, the Almighty provides us with our raison d'être. It seems natural for a rabbi to find her reason for being in the telling of stories about God. Yet everyone's life work can be sparked by the same sacred impulse. Whether or not we have a defined understanding of God, spirit moves us when we engage in our life's calling.

Doesn't the artist, in her quest for beauty or insight or revelation on a canvas or in a sculptural form, live to tell about God? Doesn't the doctor, who uses his brainpower and manual dexterity to activate the healing abilities of the sick, live to tell about God? Doesn't the lawyer, who defends people in a democratic system of justice, live to tell about God? Granted, some individuals in these professions make little use of their callings, but those who do catalyze their Divine spark into something useful, something that touches the transcendent.

Not only can we find meaning and joy in our callings, we can find meaning and joy in the ordinary events of the day. Especially when we are sick, we can learn to savor the simple pleasures: time with children or grandchildren, the smell of fresh air, the emotional power of great art or literature, the hearty laughs with a spouse or friend, the sights to behold on a summer day. These are reasons to cultivate our fighting spirit. And when we recover, we can hold on to this lesson and treasure our moments of health with a special sweetness. As Psalm 118 says, "This is the day that the Lord has made—let us exult and rejoice on it."

PSALM 121

◆ ◆ ◆

TO PLACE OUR TRUST
IN GOD'S SAFEKEEPING

The Lord will guard your going and coming

now and forever.

TO PLACE OUR TRUST
IN GOD'S SAFEKEEPING

PSALM 121

◆　◆　◆

I turn my eyes to the mountains;
*   from where will my help come?*
My help comes from the Lord,
*   maker of heaven and earth.*
He will not let your foot give way;
*   your guardian will not slumber;*
See, the guardian of Israel
*   neither slumbers nor sleeps!*
The Lord is your guardian,
*   the Lord is your protection*
*   at your right hand.*
By day the sun will not strike you,
*   nor the moon by night.*
The Lord will guard you from all harm;
*   He will guard your life.*
The Lord will guard your going and coming
*   now and forever.*

The Psalmist is in trouble. Perhaps he is ill and full of despair, fearful that he'll never get well. He looks out the window and sees the mountains in the distance. When he was well, he used to gaze at those mountains, admiring their splendor and grandeur. But he can't really appreciate them now. Instead, he keeps asking himself, "How will I recover my health? From where will my help come?" As he gazes at the mountains, his eyes half-closed, he is suddenly struck by the thought, "Of course, my help will come from God. He fashioned those mountains and so much more. He created heaven and earth."

The Psalmist realizes that the God who created the mountains is concerned for all His creations, full of compassion for every being made in His image. He is comforted by this thought; it leads him to feel that God will not ignore him, will not let him stumble. God will watch over him and care for him always, even as he endures the vicissitudes of the life of the body.

When we are ill, at home or in the hospital, abject fear can hold our hearts hostage. The nights are often the worst part of our ordeal. We can't sleep, and in the darkness every fear becomes magnified, every twinge and pain can evoke panic. We wonder from where our help will come in the midst of crisis.

In Psalm 121, the fearful Psalmist remembers that God never sleeps. God's loving presence is always there, watching over him day and night. God will protect him, His right hand always there to give him strength. God will get him through the night, remaining present so that his night fears vanish as the dawn breaks.

The pagans used the mountain as a sacred symbol, since its lofty stature on the horizon suggested a closeness to the deity. "From where will my help come?" The Psalmist turns his eyes to the mountains. In Buddhist practices, the mountain often signifies that which is timeless and trustworthy. Clouds roll by; the rain pours down; the sun is hidden, then breaks through; but the mountain stands forever, unchanged. Our own spirits, and God's presence, are as changeless and eternal as the mountain.

"The Lord will guard you from all harm." Can God really ward off illness, loss, disappointment, and tragedy? Not really. But we find an answer in the familiar traditional text of this Psalm: "He will guard your soul." God may not grant us bodies that are ageless and indomitable. But He has instilled souls that are ageless and indomitable. God can safeguard our souls even as our bodies are damaged, suffer, regenerate, or deteriorate.

I recall one member of my congregation, Stanley, an elderly man with severe chest pain who was told by his cardiologist that he needed coronary bypass surgery. In the week before his surgery, Stanley became increasingly agitated and fearful. In an effort to allay his fears, his doctor described the specifics of the surgery, which only served to exacerbate his anxiety, now bordering on panic. His wife, family, and friends tried their best to calm him by explaining that his surgery would be performed by a top-flight medical team, but their efforts were for naught.

Finally, in desperation, Stanley's wife, Carol, called to tell me about Stanley's fears as the day of surgery approached. It had gotten so bad that he would not sign the permission form for surgery, and he told his doctor that he wanted to leave the hospital. Carol knew that I had recently undergone the same operation, and even though I was still in the early stages of my own convalescence and was not yet making hospital visits, she asked whether I would make an exception to visit Stanley. I told her that I would, and I went to see him the next day.

Stanley's face brightened as I walked into his hospital room. I shared my own experience with coronary bypass, admitting that I had been quite uncomfortable for the first week or two after surgery, but that I was beginning to feel much stronger and was planning to resume my full schedule within a few weeks. I no longer had chest pain, and the doctors expected my complete recovery. Stanley listened attentively, but I could see the anxiety written all over his face. I knew that he was a religious man, so I chose to read Psalm 121 to him aloud. I asked Stanley to repeat with me the last two verses: "The Lord will guard you from all harm; He will guard your soul. The Lord will guard your going and coming now and forever."

I wrote these verses on a card, and I asked Stanley whether he would consider reading and reciting them every day until his surgery and again just before the operation itself. He thanked me for the visit, we embraced, and then we said a prayer together for his speedy recovery. As I left his room, he said that he wanted to think about my suggestion. The next day, Carol called to tell me that Stanley had signed the permission form because he felt reassured by our visit that God would be with him.

The day before his surgery, I called Stanley, and we read Psalm 121 together. "Rabbi," he said afterward, "you and God and I are an unbeatable team, and I think I'm going to make it." Stanley's surgery was successful and his recovery was smooth. He lived for another 6 years free of chest pain and other symptoms of angina. His physician told his family that those years were a gift, because without surgery his chances of survival had been slim and he would have been completely incapacitated by severe chest pain and breathlessness.

I am sure that I was able to help assuage Stanley's fears because I had undergone the same surgery, and he saw for himself that I was on the mend. But I am equally certain that Psalm 121, with its eloquent message of God's protective presence, reassured Stanley that the Almighty would be at his side throughout his ordeal.

God can help us in our struggle to cope with whatever befalls us. In illness, God bolsters our determination to get well, to fight for recovery, and to accept circumstances that we cannot control. In the face of loss, God gives us strength to grieve, then assuages our grief and plants within us the hope that our wounds will heal. In the aftermath of tragedy, He gives us the courage to remain undefeated, to emerge from our anguish without having our spirits decimated. Safeguarding our souls, God helps us recognize that we can go on living—not as a shell of our former selves, but with a newfound ability to care for ourselves and others, to live our lives fully and creatively.

God's loving-kindness, His eternal care, is with us when we get up in the morning and when we go to sleep at night, when we leave our homes to work and when we return, when we are born and during our final sentient moments. The final verse of Psalm 121 offers an infinite form of comfort: "The Lord will guard your going and coming now and forever."

PSALM 126

◆ ◆ ◆

TO REAP JOY FROM CRISIS

They who sow in tears

shall reap with songs

of joy.

TO REAP JOY FROM CRISIS

PSALM 126

◆ ◆ ◆

When the Lord restores the fortunes of Zion
    —we see it as in a dream—
    our mouths shall be filled with laughter,
    our tongues, with songs of joy.
Then shall they say among the nations,
    "The Lord has done great things for them!"
The Lord will do great things for us
    and we shall rejoice.

Restore our fortunes, O Lord,
    like watercourses in the Negeb [the dry land].
They who sow in tears
    shall reap with songs of joy.
Though he goes along weeping,
    carrying the seed-bag,
    he shall come back with songs of joy,
    carrying his sheaves.

We may perceive the suffering of illness or trauma as pointless, senseless, or meaningless. But does it have to be? Without romanticizing the anguish, can we find something worthwhile or lasting or transforming in the experience? The Psalmist affirms that we can: "They who sow in tears shall reap with songs of joy." Of course, Psalm 126 does not directly refer to illness but it surely encompasses the range of human suffering. Whether the sufferer is an exile from the Promised Land, a wanderer searching for home, a farmer whose labors are onerous, or a sick person displaced from his "normal" life, he or she can come back from the intolerable experience "with songs of joy."

With regard to illness, this may mean a full recovery and all the bliss and gratitude that accompanies it. Or it may mean a return to our spiritual home, one of unity with our loved ones and our God, one in which we are capable of peacefulness and unbridled joy. Either way, in Psalm 126, our very tears make possible the renewal to come. The sufferer who "goes along weeping" is "carrying the seed-bag" that enables him to "come back with songs of joy."

The image of sowing in tears conjures something central to the illness experience.

Often, the joy of recovery involves sheer relief, the relaxation that comes when pain gives way to pleasure, when solitude yields to sociability, when productivity replaces passivity. But it can be more than that. We may gain something new through the illness experience, and we bring it back with us.

The suffering is neither noble nor desirable, but it can put us bluntly in touch with parts of ourselves that yearn for realization and release. In times of terror, sorrow, or bewilderment, we may turn to our highest selves and our deepest faith to uncover who we are and what we hold sacred. As this process culminates—regardless of whether we emerge unscathed, with scars, or with obstinately sick bodies—we are newly rapturous and grateful for the lives we have right now.

In *A Leg to Stand On*, the renowned neurologist Oliver Sacks, M.D., writes about his own encounter with illness and infirmity. Dr. Sacks had climbed a desolate mountain in Norway when he was confronted by a rampaging bull. In his effort to escape, he badly damaged his left leg, which required extensive, complex surgery. Afterward, he went through a period of 12 days in which he could neither feel nor move his leg. During this time, he experienced his leg as alien, no longer a part of his body. Here's how Dr. Sacks describes this period: "This limbo—which lasted for 12 timeless days—started as torment, but turned into patience, started as hell, but became a purgatorial dark night, humbled me, horribly, took away hope, but sweetly-gently, returned it to me thousandfold, transformed."

Dr. Sacks describes how this "hideous and unspeakable hell" turned into "something utterly, mysteriously different—a night no longer abominable and dark, but radiant, with a light above sense—and with this, a curious, paradoxical joy. . . . "

What turns an unspeakable hell into "a curious, paradoxical joy"? The answer differs for each one of us, but certain aspects are almost universal, including a deeper immersion in our highest selves; a more rigorous search for meaning; an abandonment of trivial pursuits; a "lightening up," in which humor is cast over everything; and a renewal of faith.

Kat Duff, a gifted writer stricken with a severe case of chronic fatigue syndrome, experienced such a transformation during the course of her illness. She explains one of her routes out of "hideous hell" in her book *The Alchemy of Illness*:

We also nourish our souls by doing those things that make us feel happy, fulfilled, or right with ourselves and the world for even one moment, no matter how sick we are. Writing has been my soul-saving activity since I have been sick, no matter how bad I felt or how poorly my mind worked, a few hours of writing left me feeling better about myself and more reconciled with my circumstances. I have always wanted to write for years, but always found reasons not to; there were bills to pay, children to raise, careers to establish, political injustices to protest . . . but beneath all these imperatives was the notion that I had nothing to say, and the conviction that I did not deserve to be happy while others were not. It has taken this illness, a few years of therapy, and the authority of midlife to erode that thinking and allow myself to write—and thrive.

Evidently, the forces of decay and destruction that operate in illness facilitate subtle, though critical, reformulations of self that give our souls a little more room to breathe. Once tensions build to a critical mass and the old order finally gives way, one is often struck by an extraordinary sense of peace, the sensation of a newfound equilibrium.

Others have said that illness enabled them to rediscover their callings or return to their spiritual home. The opening verse of Psalm 126 refers to the return of the Jews from

Zion after their exile following the destruction of the First Temple. "When the Lord restores the fortunes of Zion— we see it as in a dream . . .": The people go back to their spiritual home, and the wonderment is so profound that it seems like a dream. "Our mouths shall be filled with laughter, our tongues, with songs of joy."

What has the Lord done? He has restored our fortunes, "like watercourses in the Negeb [the dry land]." It is as powerful a healing image as one can find in the Psalter. With so much desert territory, Israel and the other countries of the Middle East are subject to droughts, and they depend on rainfall for the survival of their crops and their people. In an ancient time and place in which people struggled for every drop of water, the prophets, poets, and Psalmists used the image of water to conjure replenishment, refreshment, and hope.

The image of water can surely conjure healing, since illness is often experienced as a drying up of our vital capacities, with long stretches spent at home or in hospital beds that feel desertlike in their timeless emptiness. After the healing process is set in motion, the return of health seems like the life-giving rush of a stream over dry land. Blood-flow, energy, strength, will, mental agility, and spiritual vitality return in mercifully welcome surges.

Psalm 126 reminds us that illness is part of the life cycle, that the pain and fear of the moment are not permanent conditions of our being. In one Jewish folktale, King Solomon wore a ring with a veiled inscription that he glanced at when times were hard. No one knew what it said until after his death, when the Hebrew phrase was revealed. Its translation was simply, "This too shall pass."

During my own experience with serious heart disease, I was reminded of the verse "They who sow in tears shall reap with songs of joy." After weeks of debility and even stark depression, I found the gradual return of my old energy and sense of purpose to be a continual source of joy. To once again taste life was to appreciate, as if for the first time, its full richness and sweetness.

I tell the sick people I counsel that they can look beyond their momentary distress and pain, hard as it may be, to the days when they "shall reap with songs of joy." When our very physical recovery is in doubt, the road is certainly harder, prompting a deeper quest for sources of fulfillment and happiness. But there, too, streams of compassion, love of self and others, and love of God can revive the spiritual dry land once and forever.